Roughing It Easy
in New England

**Outdoor Adventures
Near Lodgings**

- **Connecticut**
- **Maine**
- **Massachusetts**
- **New Hampshire**
- **Rhode Island**
- **Vermont**

Larry B. Pletcher

WILDERNESS PRESS
BERKELEY

FIRST EDITION July 1998

Copyright © 1998 by Larry B. Pletcher

Photos by the author unless otherwise noted
Maps by the author and Ben Pease
Design by Kathy Morey
Cover design by Larry Van Dyke
Cover photo: Newport Bay, Acadia National Park, Copyright © 1998 by Larry Ulrich

Library of Congress card catalog number 98-9395
International Standard Book Number 0-89997-210-1

Manufactured in the United States
Published by **Wilderness Press**
       2440 Bancroft Way
       Berkeley, CA 94704
       (800) 443-7227
       FAX (510) 548-1355
       wpress@ix.netcom.com

       Contact us for a free catalog
       Visit our web site at www.wildernesspress.com

Library of Congress Cataloging-in-Publication Data

Pletcher, Larry, 1946–
    Roughing it easy in New England : outdoor adventures near lodgings : Connecticut, Maine, Massachusetts, New Hampshire, Rhode Island, Vermont / Larry B. Pletcher. -- 1st ed.
        p.   cm.
    Includes bibliographical references and index.
    ISBN 0-89997-210-1
    1. Outdoor recreation--New England--Guidebooks. 2. New England--Guidebooks. I. Title.

GV199.42.N38P54   1998
917.404'43--dc21   98-9395
                                            CIP

Contents

Map Legend vi
Table of Features vii
Introduction 1
  Exploring New England 1
  Getting started — what to expect and things you'll need 2
  New England weather — learning to cope 3
  Wildlife, large and small 4
  Protecting the environment, respecting the land 5
Connecticut 7
  1. The Litchfield Hills 7
  2. Selden Neck State Park 13
Maine 18
  3. Acadia National Park 18
  4. Loon Lodge and Allagash Lake 24
  5. Chesuncook Lake House 30
  6. Cobscook Bay State Park and Moosehorn National Wildlife
    Refuge 36
  7. Daicey Pond 40
  8. Monhegan Village 44
  9. Sheepscot and Quahog Bays 49
Massachusetts 53
  10. Bascom Lodge 53
  11. Cape Cod National Seashore 59
  12. Mohawk Trail and Savoy Mountain State Forests 65
New Hampshire 69
  13. Cardigan Lodge 69
  14. The Connecticut River 75
  15. Gray Knob and Crag Camp 81
  16. Guyot Shelter 86
  17. The Hut at Madison Spring 92
  18. The Monadnock Region 97
  19. Phillips Brook Backcountry Recreation Area 103
  20. Lake Umbagog and Lake Umbagog National Wildlife Refuge . 107
  21. The Hut at Zealand Falls 112
Rhode Island 117
  22. Old Harbor 117
Vermont 124
  23. The Battenkill River 124
  24. Camel's Hump State Park 130
  25. The Catamount Trail 135
  26. The Cold Hollow Mountains 141
  27. Craftsbury Common 145
  28. The Northern Frontier 149
  29. Seyon Recreation Area 154
  30. Skyline Lodge 157
Index 162

MAP LEGEND

ROADS AND TRAILS

Other   Described
Routes   Routes

Interstate Highway

Highway

Local Road

Unpaved Road

Trail

(91)   Interstate Highways

(7)   U.S. Highways

(6A)(4)   State and Provincial Highways

FR 59   Forest Road

A   Appalachian Trail

POINTS OF INTEREST

(P)   Parking and Trailheads

×   Summits

▲   Campgrounds

◯ ○   Towns and Villages

▪   Buildings

Lighthouses

Fire Towers

∩   Covered Bridges

Parks

State Lines

WATER

Rivers and Streams

Major Rivers

Waterfalls and Cascades

Lakes and Ponds

Wetlands and Marshes

LOCATION MAPS

★   State Capitol

▪   Map Location

Table of Features

To help you decide which trips you prefer, this table shows what features are found on each trip.

State/Trip No. & Name	Inn/B&B	Backcountry Lodge	Cabin/Shelter	Campsite	Hiking	Biking	Crosscountry Skiing	Canoeing/Kayaking	Fishing	Short Walks	Swimming	Summit Views
Connecticut												
1 Litchfield Hills	•			•	•	•			•			
2 Selden Neck	•			•				•			•	
Maine												
3 Acadia Nat'l. Park	•			•	•	•	•			•	•	•
4 Loon, Allagash		•		•	•			•	•		•	•
5 Chesuncook	•			•				•	•	•		
6 Cobscook, Moosehorn			•	•	•	•		•	•	•		
7 Daicey Pond			•		•	•		•	•	•	•	•
8 Monhegan	•				•					•		
9 Sheepscot, Quahog	•							•	•	•	•	
Massachusetts												
10 Bascom Lodge		•		•	•		•			•		•
11 Cape Cod	•				•	•			•	•	•	
12 Mohawk and Savoy			•	•	•	•	•		•	•	•	•
New Hampshire												
13 Cardigan Lodge		•		•	•		•				•	•
14 Connecticut River	•			•				•	•		•	
15 Gray Knob, Crag Camp		•	•	•	•							•
16 Guyot Shelter			•	•	•							•
17 Madison Spring		•		•	•							•
18 Monadnock Region	•				•	•	•				•	•
19 Phillips Brook		•	•		•	•	•		•	•		
20 Lake Umbagog				•				•	•	•		
21 Zealand Falls		•		•	•		•				•	•
Rhode Island												
22 Old Harbor	•				•	•			•	•	•	
Vermont												
23 Battenkill	•							•	•	•		
24 Camel's Hump			•	•	•							•
25 Catamount Trail	•						•					
26 Cold Hollow	•				•					•		
27 Craftsbury	•					•	•				•	•
28 Northern Frontier	•						•					
29 Seyon Rec. Area		•			•				•	•	•	•
30 Skyline Lodge			•	•	•							•

Read This

Hiking in the backcountry entails unavoidable risk that every hiker assumes and must be aware of and respect. The fact that a trail is described in this book is not a representation that it will be safe for you. Trails vary greatly in difficulty and in the degree of conditioning and agility one needs to enjoy them safely. On some hikes routes may have changed or conditions may have deteriorated since the descriptions were written. Also, trail conditions can change even from day to day, owing to weather and other factors. A trail that is safe on a dry day or for a highly conditioned, agile, properly equipped hiker may be completely unsafe for someone else or unsafe under adverse weather conditions.

You can minimize your risks on the trail by being knowledgeable, prepared, and alert. There is not space in this book for a general treatise on safety in the mountains, but there are a number of good books and public courses on the subject, and you should take advantage of them to increase your knowledge. Just as important, you should always be aware of your own limitations and of conditions existing when and where you are hiking. If conditions are dangerous, or if you are not prepared to deal with them safely, choose a different hike! It's better to have wasted a drive than to be the subject of a mountain rescue.

These warnings are not intended to scare you off the trails. Millions of people have safe and enjoyable hikes every year. However, one element of the beauty, freedom, and excitement of the wilderness is the presence of risks that do not confront us at home. When you hike you assume those risks. They can be met safely, but only if you exercise your own independent judgment and common sense.

Introduction

Exploring New England

From alpine summits to ocean shores, from backcountry lakes to wilderness zones, the alluring New England I knew in years past still beckons outdoor enthusiasts to active recreation. *Roughing It Easy* is designed for baby-boomers like myself, who continue to love the verdant hills and hidden valleys of this extraordinary region, but would like to explore its varied treasures with a little less stress and a lot more comfort than we experienced in our youth. Ignore all memories of heavy packs, leaky tents, sketchy hygiene, and freeze-dried food. From the fog-bound coast of downeast Maine to the hills of the Nutmeg State, *Roughing It Easy* presents 30 destinations where active travelers can immerse themselves in spectacular natural settings while still enjoying a comfortable bunk, a warm meal, secure shelter, and easy backcountry access.

Most people hold memories of soaring peaks, crashing surf, and freshwater streams that make the Northeast special, but few realize how readily the New England backcountry can be enjoyed. Whether you're an outdoor beginner, an experienced hand, or a parent with energetic children, forests, mountains, rivers, and shores are accessible to active travelers along with a touch of comfort. *Roughing It Easy* describes treks through northern woodlands, hikes along mountain streams, float trips on wilderness rivers, climbs above timberline, bike rides to scenic villages, and ski paths through rural New England especially suited to people who, because of age, commitments, or condition, are no longer attracted to the opportunities described in other guides.

Each chapter of *Roughing It Easy* portrays a different adventure, beginning with an *...at a glance* glimpse at the destination and ending with a **Practical guide** that includes precise directions, useful addresses, map sources, and all information needed to make specific plans. Bountiful photos, reliable maps, and engaging, lively descriptions evoke the distinctive qualities of every varied region and convey a compelling sense of actually being there. Each chapter guides readers to an exciting, user-friendly destination: a lakeside cabin with views of Katahdin, a campsite served by water taxi on a large wilderness lake, a historic inn reached by canoe in the wilds of Thoreau's Maine, or a comfortable hut perched on a ridge among towering White Mountain peaks.

New England's impressive array of ecological regions is captured in *Roughing It Easy* trips that invite hikers, bikers, boaters, and adventurers to sample the brilliant spectrum of nature that enriches the New England states. Paddle a river through the New Hampshire hills, stroll by the sea on a Rhode Island bluff, ski inn to inn in northern Vermont, or retreat to a solitary cabin deep in the Massachusetts woods. *Roughing It Easy* presents an exceptional assortment of remote outdoor adventures that beckon readers to savor one or more comfortable days exploring the bounties of nature in this special corner of our land.

Getting started — what to expect and things you'll need

Dry bunks and warm meals don't remove the risk from wilderness travel. Several of the destinations included in *Roughing It Easy* guide readers through backcountry regions where personal safety is strictly up to you. For safe adventures, use common sense, expect the unexpected, and plan to pack gear that stands up to the worst conditions a region may offer. Select outings that match your level of fitness, don't push beyond your limits, and be sure you have basic skills that might be needed if you encounter adverse conditions.

For a rapid assessment of any outing listed in *Roughing It Easy*, check the *...at a glance* section at the start of each chapter. Each destination is rated as Easy, Moderate, or Rough to reflect its physical challenge and the degree of preparation involved. In *...at a glance* you'll also find a brief description of how to reach your destination, the type of lodging provided, and a quick capsule summary of the natural highlights that any visitor can find.

"Easy" trips are natural choices for families with younger children and newcomers to a sport. Only basic gear and minimal conditioning are required. For hikes in this category, comfortable walking shoes and a small day pack are generally all you'll need. For bikers, boaters, or skiers, the basic equipment of each sport should be enough to get you by.

"Moderate" trips enter more rugged terrain beyond the reach of immediate help in the event you get into trouble. Active people in fair condition will enjoy a spirited workout. Smokers and people out of condition will still, no doubt, get by, but will feel that they're pushing their limits. At this level, hikers require sturdy boots and a pack with foul-weather gear, while bikers and skiers should carry the tools and equipment needed to make repairs.

"Rough" outings are exactly as the term implies, extended trips through remote, difficult terrain where prolonged effort, steep trails, or demanding conditions are all part of the fun. Trips in this category are definitely not for beginners. People who are reasonably fit should have a great adventure, but weekend warriors in only fair shape may face a very long day. On long, strenuous trips, wool mittens, a wool cap, and a fleece jacket should find their way into your pack, especially if you plan to wander onto New England's highest peaks.

Above all, don't attempt any trip that's clearly beyond your limits, and don't hesitate to turn around if your inner voice whispers that you're getting in over your head. Hiking alpine trails, canoeing wild rivers, skiing remote terrain, and kayaking off the coast are terrific action sports but only for experienced people who have learned the needed skills. Before tackling any new challenge, check the end of its chapter for specific sources of further information, travel with a knowledgeable group, or seek professional instruction.

From crudely rustic to casually elegant, the *...at a glance* guide at the head of each chapter also reveals the comfort level of **Accommodations** that you'll find. In many cases, a single destination offers a mix of lodging options or a chance to link inn to inn on exciting overland treks. Check **The practical guide** at the end of each chapter for details on reservations and more specific information regarding accommodations. For rustic listings, **The practical guide** will let readers know whether sleeping bags are needed, what's supplied for sheets and towels, and whether guests must supply their meals.

New England weather — learning to cope

Year after year the New England states are blessed with four reliable seasons of very different weather. Day by day, however, prevailing conditions aren't so easy to predict. In the middle of August, howling winds and stinging sleet can pester the highest northern peaks, while hikers in southern areas might find bare ground for walks at Christmas time. Only change is certain. The best defense is to expect the unexpected, and consider the quirky climate just part of the outdoor challenge.

Winter conditions may be the most difficult to predict. January might bring sub-zero cold, bitter winds and little measurable snow, or deep blue skies, clear air, and a thick blanket of white. Cross-country ski treks in *Roughing It Easy* are located in regions where the average winter delivers reliable snow, but where temperatures will also be quite severe. Dress in wool or synthetic fleece, and be sure to layer your clothing.

Spring in New England brings mud season, that bothersome time of year when snows have melted, skies stay grey, and the ground refuses to dry. Mud season is a good time to stay off mountain trails, but the date of its arrival is impossible to predict. In northern New England, St. Patrick's day may dawn clear and balmy, yet April flowers can be rudely squelched by a sheath of heavy snow. Sooner or later, of course, the hardships of mud season end and spring offers a fleeting chance to enjoy its unique rewards before the hatch of summer bugs: warm, fragrant days when the pastel buds of the hardwood forests emerge with a pale glow that signals a fresh beginning of another outdoor year.

Predictable by New England standards, summer remains the most popular outdoor season. Hot, humid, sweltering weather is rare in these northern climes. Warm days, moderate humidity, and cool nights remain the general rule, ideal conditions for exploring wild terrain. Still, a few cautions are in order. Crystal blue mornings can quickly become stormy afternoons. For boaters and high-peak hikers, being your own weather forecaster is a risky proposition. Thunderstorms sweep across mountain ridges at frighteningly rapid speeds and gusty winds turn quiet afternoons on large lakes into heart pounding races to shore. Check local weather forecasts, stay alert for sudden changes, and use extra caution whenever you venture into an exposed position.

From cranberry bogs to mountain tops, the brilliant colors of Autumn announce the premier New England season. Blazing maples, golden ferns, and the muted tones of marsh and heather cloak the landscape with luminous hues that complement a crisp, clear sky. Beginning in mid-September along the Canadian border and sweeping south to Connecticut in the glorious days of late October, a gaudy display dazzles outdoor enthusiasts who flock here by the thousands from all around the world. You'll be enchanted if you join the crowds, but savvy visitors also know that autumn is the perfect time to explore those marvelous places that are packed with people at the height of summer. From Cape Cod to the wilds of Maine, solitary wanderers who aren't opposed to paddling streams or combing shores while wearing a light fall jacket discover that autumn is the best of times for roughing it in New England.

Wildlife, large and small

Quaint villages, rocky shores, and marvelous alpine peaks are common images of rural New England, but moose, eagles, seals, and whales might just as readily come to mind. Throughout the Northeast, opportunities for spotting wildlife are plentiful and quite diverse. For best results, stay away from postcard settings and picturesque mountaintops. You'll have better luck in little-known fields and forests throughout this six-state region that quietly furnish food and cover for abundant wildlife.

Moose are popular attractions for visitors to northern regions where these lanky, nearsighted denizens range from marshy swamps to forested hills. Throughout Maine and northern New Hampshire, plentiful moose have even created a hazard on rural roads by nonchalantly veering into the paths of speeding cars. Slow down if you spot one by the side of the road, even if you don't plan to stop and watch it for awhile.

Black bear also frequent many New England forests. Though usually not aggressive except when protecting their young, omnivorous bears naturally scrounge for food. Backcountry campers should bear-proof their food supply by hanging it between trees or storing it in the bear-proof containers that are sometimes provided in established sites.

Visitors to the backcountry may be lucky enough to spot any number of other mammals: deer, fox, raccoon, squirrel, coyote, otter, and fisher are common creatures of the New England woods. Seals and even whales on rare occasions may be seen from coastal locations, and birders will espe-

A common sight in the North Maine woods

cially enjoy several stops along the Atlantic Flyway.

Regrettably, visitors to this region are far more likely to come into contact with much smaller creatures. Mosquitoes and black flies are responsible for a reign of terror that peaks in a rolling wave from south to north in early May through mid-July. Mosquitoes, of course, love standing water and particularly coastal marshes, while black flies hatch in running streams and venture forth to torment man and beast with a nasty bite that bleeds. Fortunately, both critters can be controlled with any good insect repellent containing "DEET," and the hazard fades, at least in the daytime, shortly after mid-July.

Two very small critters carry the potential for serious consequences. *Giardia lamblia* is a waterborne parasite that may be present in any surface water in the northeastern United States. Do not drink water from lakes, streams, or similar sources without filtration, boiling for five minutes, or other adequate treatment. Throughout New England, but especially in Connecticut, Massachusetts, and Rhode Island, including Block Island and the coastal zones, deer ticks carry Lyme disease. Flu-like symptoms and the distinctive bull's-eye rash can lead to long-term disabling illness if untreated. Fortunately, the pinhead-sized ticks must remain on your body for many hours in order to transmit the disease. In tick-prone areas, wear long pants tucked into your socks, spray with repellent containing "DEET," do a body check after exposure, and remove ticks with tweezers if any are found.

Protecting the environment, respecting the land

In an era when heavy use threatens to appreciate nature to death, the golden rule of "Pack It In/Pack It Out" must be honored by all who explore this beautiful country. If visitors apply a few basic principles, none of the trails, beach-side paths, or bodies of water in *Roughing It Easy* will be harmed. Carry a small trash bag in your pack and pick up after yourself. Most people seem to have gotten the message. Candy wrappers and bits of plastic less frequently blight our trails, and concerned friends of the environment take the extra step of carrying out more than they carried in.

Whether losing yourself for a few mellow days hiking a backwoods trail or taking a break for a short afternoon strolling an ocean shore, walk lightly and respect the land. In the mud of early spring, conscientious hikers completely avoid steep slopes and unstable routes. Several trips in *Roughing It Easy* takes readers to regions that are exceptionally sensitive to human intrusion. On alpine peaks, on Cape Cod dunes, or in the vicinity of nesting sites, it's critical to obey posted closures and step only on established paths. Resist the urge to pester wildlife, and keep a respectful distance. Boaters should steer clear of beach-front rookeries, and canoeists on large lakes should stay away from nesting loons. In some cases, rare and fragile alpine flowers lurk within inches of mountain trails. Tucked between rocks or carpeting vast alpine lawns, these delicate plants tolerate the frigid gales of a windswept peak, but may never recover from the weight of a misplaced boot. Visitors to the backcountry have a special obligation to preserve and protect the creations of nature that draw them to these regions. While you enjoy the treasures of New England, walk with respect and please stay on the trail.

Connecticut

1. The Litchfield Hills

Kent, Sharon, and West Cornwall, Connecticut

The Litchfield Hills at a glance

Destination: A 37-mile bicycle tour through the hills of western Connecticut
Location: Near Kent, about 24 miles north of Danbury
Access: A combination of paved and gravel roads
Difficulty: Moderate
Accommodations: Drive-in campsites or comfortable country inns
Duration: One day with overnight options
Featured attractions: Macedonia Brook, the Housatonic River, and unexpected wildlife

A link between mountains and sea, and a place where New England deftly evolves from urban megalopolis to rural hamlet and town, Connecticut is a state of transition. The quaint villages, stylish homes, and well-preserved open spaces of the beautiful Litchfield Hills represent the Nutmeg State at its best. Along the banks of the Housatonic River or in the folds of its gentle hills, this 37-mile bicycle tour wanders well off the beaten path to thoroughly explore every aspect of Connecticut's country mode. Two state parks, a state forest, a covered bridge, an art colony, a National Audubon sanctuary, picturesque farms, the Appalachian Trail, and a town common rimmed by stately homes highlight this sophisticated jaunt, which rewards outdoor enthusiasts with white-water rivers, meandering streams, sequestered woods, and unexpected wildlife.

Whether you plan to camp at a streamside site or relax in a country inn, your visit should begin in Kent, a historic town that transformed itself from an early manufacturing center to a home for contemporary art. Galleries, shops, restaurants, and bed-and-breakfast inns line U.S. Highway 7 north of the center of town, a comfortable base of operations for exploring the Housatonic Valley and the surrounding Litchfield Hills.

Visitors who stay in town can bike from the heart of the village, but campers — and bicyclists who would like to shave a few miles off their trip — should continue by car 5.1 miles north to Macedonia Brook State Park. From the stop light in the middle of Kent, ride or drive west on Highway 341, quickly crossing the Housatonic River and the path of the Appala-

Pedaling a Connecticut backroad in Macedonia Brook State Park

chian Trail. Entering the district where a town forest fueled an iron forge in the early 1800s, you'll rapidly leave the 20th Century as you ease out of the valley and turn right onto Macedonia Brook Road only 1.7 miles from the center of town. The first of several gravel roads encountered on this tour, this ancient lane offers few reminders of modern life as it climbs steadily north, bears left at Fuller Mountain Road, and leads upstream to the headquarters of Macedonia Brook State Park.

Picnic tables and easily accessible campsites dot the banks of a plunging stream that skims past the foot of Cobble Mountain in this 2300-acre park. Crisscrossing the gravel lane and weaving through the camps, the waters of this tumbling brook nourish a channel of emerald glades while spring beauties and violets brighten nearby forest and field. Hiking trails to mountain views and countless white cascades enhance Macedonia's drive-in campsites, a fine introduction to Connecticut's wonders for cyclists who stop for the night or pedalers just passing through.

Beneath towering hardwoods near the north end of the park, a four-way junction of gravel roads marks the beginning and end of a 27-mile loop, and also supplies space for a car if you've driven here from Kent. To start a clockwise circuit, pedal northwest on Weber Road as it leaves this intersection and quickly discovers Hilltop Pond after rising to exit the park. Pause for a brief overview near the outlet of this man-made lake before skirting the damp lowlands that line the nearest shore and provide a favored habitat for deer and Canada geese. Weber Road is paved beyond the pond, which is just before you find that its name changes to Knibloc Hill Road only 1.1 mile from your start. Prepare for a speedy descent! Knibloc Hill becomes a long brake-testing glide with views of hills and dairy farms as it drops into a fertile valley.

At the bottom of Knibloc Hill, turn right onto Highway 41 within sight of Hitchcock Corners, where a traffic island on the New York border is a remnant of a town divided when boundaries were drawn in 1731. Bear right through this three-sided junction, joining Highway 41 on a 4.4-mile ride past fields of black-and-white cattle and farms with bright red barns. Rolling along the contours of a gentle valley, this rural jaunt reminds you that you're in the country by sampling the sweet aroma of lilacs, the sour smell of silage, and the pungent scent of dairy barns.

Cow pastures give way to stately homes as you enter Sharon, a quiet crossroads town with a village green that's more than 260 years old. Immaculate and well preserved, the historic district affords a small cafe to satisfy your hunger and ample space to stretch your legs before deciding to move on. Pass through the intersection with Highway 343 near the south end of the common, continue 0.6 mile north through the middle of town, and turn right at the junction with Calkinstown Road at the Sharon Motor Lodge.

Calkinstown Road presents the first uphill challenge of the day, but guides you back to natural surroundings. A long, moderate climb leads past rural homes and reaches a divide between watersheds after 1.5 miles. Continue straight at the junction with Jackson Road, bear right at White Hollow Road, and follow the direction of Calkinstown Road as its name changes to West Cornwall Road. Dropping rapidly to angle across a valley of broad wetlands circled by wooded hills, West Cornwall Road skirts the Emily Winthrop Miles Wildlife Sanctuary on your right and the Roy Swamp Wildlife Management Area on your left. Between these National Audubon and Connecticut state sanctuaries are likely spots for listening to songbirds, admiring a beaver lodge, or peering among tangled reeds for black ducks and mergansers.

Footbridge over Macedonia Brook

Rimmed by beaver-chewed stumps and throbbing with the twang of frogs, the wetland preserve continues to shadow the right side of the highway as the pavement rises about 20 feet along the edge of a hill. Wildflowers and wildlife viewing highlight these easy miles, as the wetlands expand to open ponds near the headquarters of the Audubon sanctuary and contract again to cattail marshes and thickets that squeeze through a gap in the hills.

West Cornwall Road leaves the marsh, tops a rise, and passes an old cemetery before commencing a roller-coaster descent that ends in West Cornwall, directly across US Highway 7 from a marvelous covered bridge. Drop off the highway and take a spin through this ancient one-way span, which leads to a bustling village that offers more than meets the eye. A deli, a bistro, a bookseller and a collection of skilled craft shops inhabit this country town. Stroll the intimate streets, eat your lunch in a shady park, and share the excitement as white-water paddlers shoot the rapids under the bridge.

The 4.3 miles of US Highway 7 from West Cornwall to the junction with Highway 4 are a stunning riverfront journey, but the busiest of your trip. Be especially cautious in the first mile of Highway 7 south where the pavement narrows between rock ledges and the banks of the Housatonic. A great, broad, rippling river unmarred on either shore creates a wonderful corridor as you follow the flow downstream. Turnouts and waterfront stops are plentiful in these scenic miles which are part of Housatonic Meadows State Park, but white-water paddlers and fishing fanatics are likely to get there first. The park entrance and overnight camps are in the middle of this downstream stretch, but better prospects for private spots to relax by the shore are a little further south.

The right turn (west) onto Highway 4 makes up for your earlier coasting, a stiff climb that moderates in only 0.7 mile after crossing the Appalachian Trail. Keep rising through a series of pitches another 1.8 miles, turn left onto West Woods Road #2, and your effort quickly eases. As with any good trip, the final 5.5 miles save the best for last. Pay close attention to street signs as West Woods Road #2 twists through intersections, especially at a corner where it turns right and immediately changes to gravel. Also stay alert as you pedal around the next blind curve. I scared a hawk as I turned the corner and confounded geese herding their goslings in a marsh by the side of the road. With no fear of a man on a bike, they milled about as I rode within 8 feet, a distance that would have made them flee had I tried to approach on foot.

Beyond the marsh, West Woods Road #2 rolls through the forest and shimmies between a house and a barn before reaching a four-way junction. Aim diagonally across this remote intersection and enter Keeler Road, a paved street that soon reverts to gravel. In this final link on an empty road you're all alone with woods, streams, and marshes. Soon enough, signs will announce that you're back in Macedonia Brook State Park at the junction with Weber Road. Go slow and enjoy the ride.

The practical guide

Access: Kent, Connecticut is on US Highway 7 between Danbury, Connecticut (Interstate 84) and the Great Barrington/Stockbridge region of western Massachusetts. All paved and gravel roads described on this circuit are suitable for family vehicles.

Cyclists should understand that gravel roads in this region are generally not a thick layer of loose stones but rather a hard-packed surface.

With annual maintenance, these gravel roads can be fairly smooth and easy to ride. Potholes and washboard surfaces often develop late in the season, but mountain bikes are not necessary during most of the riding year.

Accommodations and reservations: In Kent and vicinity: The Country Goose Bed and Breakfast, 211 Kent-Cornwall Road, Kent, CT 06757, Tel. (860) 927-4746; The Gibbs House Bed and Breakfast, 87 North Main Street, Kent, CT 06757, Tel. (860) 927-1754; Fife'n Drum Inn and Restaurant, 53 North Main Street, Kent, CT 06757, Tel. (860) 927 3509;

In Sharon: 1890 Colonial Bed & Breakfast, Route 41, P.O. Box 25, Sharon, CT 06069, Tel. (860) 364-0436; The Sharon Motor Lodge, Route 41, Sharon, CT 06069, Tel. (860) 364-0462.

For camping at Macedonia Brook State Park or Housatonic Meadows State Park contact the Connecticut State Parks Division at the address given below.

Maps: Connecticut Bicycle Map, Connecticut Department of Transportation, 2800 Berlin Turnpike, P.O. Box 317546, Newington, CT 06131-7546.

Topographic county maps, Connecticut Department of Environmental Protection, Natural Resource Center, 165 Capitol Ave., Room 555, Hartford, CT 06106, Tel. (860) 566-3540.

For further information: State Parks Division, Bureau of Outdoor Recreation, Department of Environmental Protection, 79 Elm Street, Hartford, CT 06106-5127, Tel. (860) 424-3200; Emily Winthrop Miles Wildlife Sanctuary, 99 West Cornwall Road, Sharon, CT 06069, Tel. (860) 364-0048.

1. THE LITCHFIELD HILLS

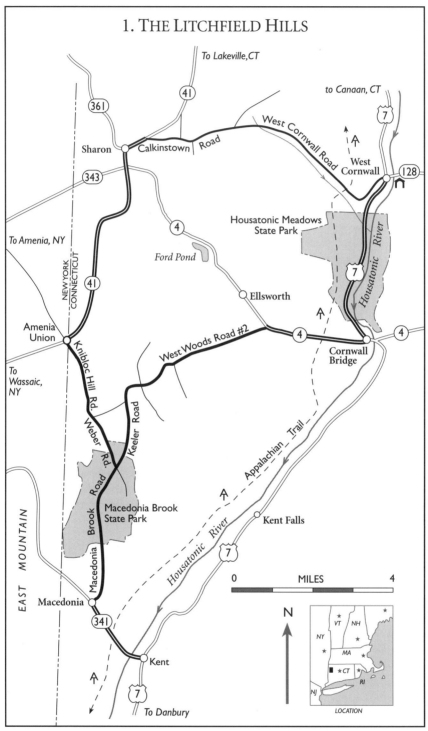

To Lakeville,CT

to Canaan, CT

41

361

7

Sharon   Calkinstown   Road

West Cornwall Road

West Cornwall

343

128

Housatonic Meadows State Park

4

Ford Pond

To Amenia, NY

Housatonic River

41

Ellsworth

7

Amenia Union

West Woods Road #2

4

4

Cornwall Bridge

To Wassaic, NY

Knibloc Hill Rd.

Keeler Road

Weber Rd.

Appalachian Trail

Macedonia Brook State Park

Brook Road

Housatonic River

Kent Falls

EAST MOUNTAIN

Macedonia

7

Macedonia

341

Kent

7

To Danbury

0   MILES   4

N

LOCATION

2. Selden Neck State Park

Deep River, Connecticut

Selden Neck at a glance

Destination: A boaters-only island park between Selden Creek and the Connecticut River

Location: About 28 miles south of Hartford

Access: Paved road to boat launch; canoe to campground and sights

Difficulty: Moderate

Accommodations: Campsite on the river or comfortable country inn

Duration: One day with overnight options

Featured attractions: Waterfront camping, rare plants, and abundant wildlife

Ebbing and flowing with the daily tides, the waters that swirl past Selden Island give the final miles of the Connecticut River a distinctly nautical flair. Only ten miles from Long Island Sound, sailing yachts and power boats dart along a buoyed channel, following a course that once sent wooden vessels to New York or Zanzibar. Shipbuilding and piano keys were the local stock in trade. Launch a canoe from the dock in Deep River, and try to imagine what it was like when 12,000 pounds of ivory landed here every month.

With the end of the ivory trade, the banks of the Connecticut River came to reflect local pastimes more hospitable to nature. Blending into a wooded landscape along the eastern shore, Selden Neck State Park lines an unspoiled waterfront, but gives no hint that it occupies an island without roads. Cut off from mainland intrusions by narrow Selden Creek, the cattail marshes and granite heights of spacious Selden Island attract local boaters and abundant wildlife. Reserved for guests who paddle canoes or navigate small craft, four campsite clusters dot this park's 1.2 miles of river frontage, private sites with relaxing views of life on the waterfront scene. A tent on Selden Island makes a great base for exploring nearby coves; just be prepared to fall asleep to the honk of squabbling geese and the splash of landing swans.

In spite of the park's many attractions, the focal point for naturalists who come to this salty

Arrival at Deep River dock

region is beautiful Selden Creek. Curling along the back side of Selden Island, this secluded tidal channel slips between cliffs and marshes, passes a Nature Conservancy preserve, and connects to the Connecticut River through coves at either end. A tour of the creek and island makes a fine one-day excursion for guests of local inns, but a campsite on the river lets paddlers discover wildlife at a special time of day. Come to these quiet waters in the stillness of a summer evening for the magical chance to trace the wake of an otter, drift the creek with a whistling swan, or follow the flight of an osprey soaring overhead.

The closest boat launch to Selden Neck State Park is in Deep River, Connecticut. From the public dock on the western shore, sight over the top of swans and gulls at the tip of Eustasia Island and you'll spot a red navigational marker directly across the river on Selden Island's shore. Two camp areas are north of this channel marker, while the Springledge and Quarry Knob sites are stationed to its south. Leaving the relative calm of the Deep River landing, paddle over the mucky shallows at the north end of Eustasia Island and head directly east. Tides and typical currents should pose no problem on this moderate river crossing, but wind and the wash of pleasure boats could give you a bit of a scare. Spot the Chester/Hadlyme ferry and imposing Gillette Castle about one mile to the north, and use caution entering the boating channel as you near the eastern shore. Bound for the Quarry Knob campsite, I turned south when I reached the island, cruising past showy dogwoods and clusters of wildflowers that capped the rocks along the bank just above the splashing tides.

Wind, weather, and larger boats govern your approach to Selden Creek. Tides and currents on this portion of the Connecticut River aren't usually strong enough to prevent canoeists from paddling against the flow, and on most days it's possible to enter Selden Creek from either end. Under typical summer conditions, then, circumnavigation of Selden Island is possible in either direction, and by sticking close to shore canoes can stay out of the boating channel for most of the 2.5-mile route. On the other hand, if brisk wind or the wash of larger boats threatens too great a challenge, you're better off reducing your time on the river by heading for the nearest inlet and paddling in both directions on the waters of the quiet creek.

A stiff breeze turned me south from Quarry Knob, pushing my canoe against a rising tide as granite hills tapered to a sandy spit at the south end of the island. Floating downstream, the first left turn enters Selden Creek, a broad, prominent channel that leaves the Connecticut River before the eastern shore rises again to the bulge of another hill. Bending back to the northeast, Selden Creek soon passes the bounds of a Nature Conservancy preserve and quickly instills a sense of solitude as it narrows to its first turn in less than 0.25 mile. Trills, whistles, the call of a red-winged blackbird high on a solo perch, and the chattered warning of a kingfisher swooping along the shore echo from low banks and from the breadth of a cattail marsh. While canoes drift slowly north, a pair of ducks dashes with apparent purpose overhead, and a father swan floats as silent sentry in front of a narrow entrance to a backwater neighborhood.

About one third of the way up the meandering channel, wetlands on the eastern shore make way for wooded hills, as Selden Creek slides past the base of granite faces that plunge to the water's edge. Intimate and oddly constricted between cliffs and spreading marsh, the channel's sides appear to contradict themselves: pines and sterile rock contrasting with fertile grasslands awash in tidal muck. It's a fine region to explore one of the side channels that twist into the marsh, or to beach your canoe on a wetland shore simply to rest for awhile and see what visiting wildlife might happen to drop by.

Wandering north beyond the halfway point, the creek slowly widens and eventually divides after passing a stone house on top of a hill to the right. Bear left when you see a boat house dead ahead, and follow the northern coast of Selden Island as it curls through a wide cove and re-joins the Connecticut River. Cruising through this watery junction, you'll have time to make a choice. If you need to end your day, continue south along the bending shore to reach the campsites on Selden Island or return to the navigational marker across from the Deep River dock. If time and weather allow, though, point your bow upstream where two variations on wetland environments are hidden behind the shore.

As you look up-river from the mouth of the northern inlet to Selden Creek, the twin docks of the Chester/Hadlyme ferry make convenient points of reference. On the right, about 0.75 mile away, just south of the ferry landing on the east side of the river, is the entrance to Whalebone Cove. Opening into a knot of twisting channels, Whalebone Creek leads to a shallow estuary where mudflats and wild rice make a popular fast-food stop for passing waterfowl and a grand site for a second Nature Conservancy preserve.

Also on the right, one mile north of the ferry landing, is the southern entrance to Chapman Pond, an unusual freshwater pool with inlet/outlet

Flatwater paddling on Selden Creek

channels that are governed by the tides. Another Nature Conservancy preserve, this expansive pond provides critical habitat for alewives and freshwater fish. Ducks, herons, or woodland mammals can often be spotted in the one-mile journey from the southern inlet to the far end of this scenic pond, while wooded uplands on the eastern shore give paddlers a chance to stretch their legs on the traces of an old town road.

On your return to Selden Island, a boat launch and picnic ground that abuts the ferry landing break up a lengthy paddle. Just avoid the wash of the ferry boat as you navigate by the dock.

The practical guide

Access: To reach the boat launch in Deep River, leave Connecticut Highway 9 at exit 6 and follow Highway 148 2.1 miles through the town of Chester to the junction with Highway 154. Turn right on Highway 154, drive south 1.5 miles, and turn left (east) onto Kirtland Street at the Rankin Family Pub. The boat launch is 0.8 mile straight ahead just across the railroad tracks near the Deep River Navigation Company. Parking at the boat launch is for town residents only. After unloading, find a place for your car a few yards away on the other side of the tracks.

An alternate launch site is adjacent to the Chester/Hadlyme ferry not far from the entrance to Gillette Castle. This historic mansion is worth a visit if only for the flower gardens and the river view from the terrace. From exit 7 of Connecticut Highway 9, follow Highway 82 as it twists and turns 5.6 miles east, crosses the Connecticut River, passes through the town of East Haddam, and finds a right turn onto River Road. All turns are marked with signs for Gillette Castle State Park. The Castle entrance is 1.6 miles south on River Road. The ferry landing and boat launch is 1.0 mile beyond the castle entrance.

From Gillette Castle, cross the river on the ferry, then drive 0.6 mile west on Connecticut Highway 148, and you've circled back to the 148/154 intersection near the town of Chester and the Deep River dock.

Accommodations and reservations: Reservations for campsites at Selden Neck State Park must be made at least two weeks before your intended stay. Written application and payment in full are required in advance. Stays are limited to one night. For information on campsite availability and camping permit applications contact Supervisor, Gillette Castle State Park, 67 River Road, East Haddam, CT 06423, Tel. (860) 526-2336.

For nearby inns try: The Inn at Chester, Route 148, 318 West Main Street, Chester, CT 06412, Tel. (860) 526-9541; Bishopsgate Inn, Goodspeed Landing, P.O. Box 290, East Haddam, CT 06423, Tel. (860) 873-1677; The Gelston House, Route 82, East Haddam, CT 06423, Tel. (860) 873-1411.

Maps: USGS Deep River quad

For further information: State of Connecticut, State Parks Division, Bureau of Outdoor Recreation, Department of Environmental Protection, 79 Elm Street, Hartford, CT 06106-5127, Tel. (860) 424-3200.

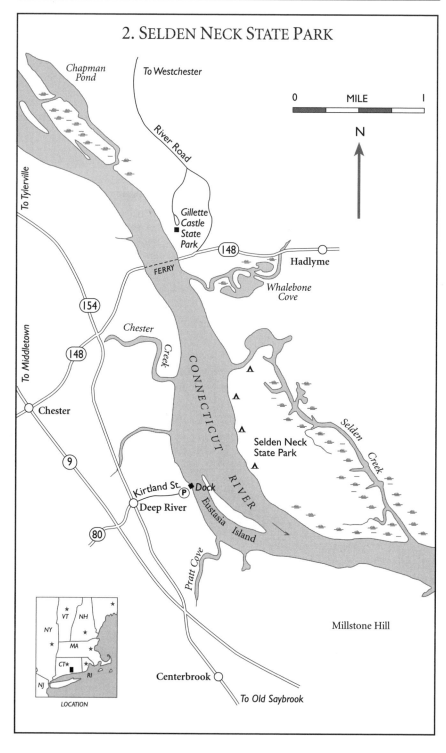

2. SELDEN NECK STATE PARK

Chapman Pond

To Westchester

River Road

0   MILE   I

N

To Tylerville

Gillette Castle State Park

148

FERRY

Hadlyme

Whalebone Cove

154

148

Chester Creek

CONNECTICUT RIVER

To Middletown

Chester

9

Selden Creek

Selden Neck State Park

Kirtland St.

P Dock

Deep River

80

Eustasia Island

Pratt Cove

Millstone Hill

VT NH

NY

MA

CT★

RI

NJ

LOCATION

Centerbrook

To Old Saybrook

3. Acadia National Park

Mount Desert Island, Maine

Acadia at a glance

Destination: New England's only national park
Location: Coastal Maine, about 40 miles southeast of Bangor
Access: Paved roads to trailheads and entrances to carriage roads
Difficulty: Options from easy to rough
Accommodations: Choices ranging from campgrounds to luxurious resort-style inns
Duration: Overnight or extended stay
Featured attractions: Cadillac Mountain, Somes Sound, Seawall, Bass Harbor Head Light, tidepools, oceanfront cliffs, and miles of carriage roads

Exploring the length of the Maine coast in the fall of 1604, Samuel de Champlain observed a high-notched island composed of seven or eight mountains rising to bare-rock summits from slopes of birch, fir, and pine. In spite of many changes over nearly 400 years, the essence of Mount Desert Island remains much the same, a magnificent appendage to the fog-bound coast of Maine with rocky shores and jagged headlands overlooking Frenchman Bay. Along with remote Schoodic Point, Baker Island, and a section of Isle au Haut, Acadia National Park encompasses much of Mount Desert Island, sharing the intricate landscape with havens for the rich and famous and the saltwater yachting crowd.

Acadia National Park displays incomparable coastal beauty, but it's also rather crowded. Endlessly fascinating to artists, lovers of tides, and walkers of foggy shores, Mount Desert Island stands as Maine's quintessential rocky coast. Beyond tidepools, wildlife, and stunning waterfront scenes, Mount Desert Island includes the only fjord on the eastern seaboard, the highest headlands north of Rio de Janeiro, and the highest point on the Atlantic coast. Comfort has long been provided to people who visit Bar Harbor, and there are ways to enjoy Acadia's wonders while escaping the summer crowds. Don't miss seeing this fabulous island just because it's so well-known.

While wave-splashed ocean shores contain the soul of this national park, roads in one form or another lie at its very heart. State highways, park roads, and historic carriage trails combine to provide unrivalled access to Acadia's scenic highlights. For a stunning introduction to the natural beauty of Mount Desert Island, begin with a drive on the Park Loop Road that's reached from various points beyond the visitor center. Unlike scenic drives in larger parks, this leisurely 20-mile circuit around a portion of the claw-shaped island provides car-bound visitors with a chance to come face to face with the best scenery in the park. Skimming the coast from the crescent cove of Sand Beach to the cliffs of Otter Point, this heavily travelled thoroughfare continues past Jordan Pond and leads to an obligatory detour to the top of Cadillac Mountain. On a clear day, you'll share the experience with hundreds of other tourists. As you sample the views of Bar Harbor, Frenchman Bay and the islands of down-east Maine, just keep in mind that opportunities to enjoy more private moments are out there to be found.

To avoid the crowds on the Park Loop Road start early in the morning, or at least understand that parking lots and turnouts don't mark every worthwhile sight. On one-way sections of this two-lane road, signs designate long stretches where parking is permitted in the right-hand lane. Take advantage of this golden opportunity to find secluded spots that most tourists miss. Merely yards from the Blackwoods Campground, busy traffic streams past the tip of Hunter Head, oblivious to one of the most striking points on the entire Acadian coast. Look for a nondescript opening in a post-and-rail fence, where a dirt path weaves down a slope through a screen of evergreens. Less than 20 feet from the pavement, granite cliffs tower above crashing surf, and views restricted only by fog look out to the open sea.

Before you abandon your car, you should also explore parts of the island that crowds tend to ignore. On the way to the southern tip of the

The rocky coast of Mount Desert Island

island and Bass Harbor Head Light, follow the state highways that circle the fjord known as Somes Sound, stopping in Somesville and Seal Harbor for a taste of village life. Picnic at Pretty Marsh, take a swim at Echo Lake, or search misty acres of tidepools on Seawall's stony shore as herring gulls keep close watch over periwinkles, rock weed, barnacles, and kelp.

After a car-bound introduction to Mount Desert Island, you'll be anxious to discover Acadia's other type of road. John D. Rockefeller, Jr., before his contribution of nearly one-third of the land that later became Acadia National Park, saw to the construction of state-of-the-art carriage trails that allowed sedate exploration of the island's rugged terrain. Between Northeast Harbor and Hull Cove, visitors still enjoy stylish horse-drawn rides, but 44 miles of these graded lanes are more appealing today to hikers, bikers, and cross-country skiers searching for quiet corners of this seaside mountain range. Following natural contours, these elaborate roads pass over arched bridges and granite retaining walls as they weave an intricate pattern of intersecting paths that lead from ponds in interior valleys to the highest rocky slopes.

Connected by a choice of looping trails, European-style gatehouses at Jordan Pond and Northeast Harbor mark entrances to a carriage-road system that quickly transports adventurous travelers away from pesky crowds. Mountain bikers will especially relish the Round Mountain Loop, which bounces through dense woodlands, crosses hiking trails, and provides glimpses of the Atlantic Ocean from verdant mountainsides. After sampling popovers and homemade ice cream at the Jordan Pond House, pedal above the floor of a deep glacial valley, curl to spectacular vistas near the top of Sargent Mountain, and plunge down the other side watching fleets of tiny sailboats on the waters of Somes Sound. Amid trickling streams, deep ravines, and views that match those from Cadillac Mountain, you'll pass few other bikers on this solitary route, which takes you to backcountry portions of an island that's not quite tame.

If your interests are strictly pedestrian, more than 140 miles of paths in Acadia National Park run the gamut from easy jaunts to ascents over rungs and ladders on the strenuous Precipice Trail. Hike to the top of a mountain, explore a nature trail, or cross the bar at low tide for access to Bar Island.

Exceptionally easy and only feet from the Park Loop Road, the Ocean Trail remains the most popular hike on Mount Desert Island, if only for the excuse to wander on cliffs and hop from rock to rock. Beginning at Sand Beach, the simple walk on the Ocean Trail leads three miles to views at Otter Point, but most hikers never get that far. Wild roses and a spicy fragrance greet walkers on these seaside cliffs. Turn away from the trail on one of the paths worn through the vegetation, and you'll find yourself standing atop multiple layered blocks of pink feldspar granite that tilt toward the sea like a landscape in a whimsical cubist painting. Gulls cry, waves crash, and the throaty roar of a fishing boat rises from the water as

Sand Beach, Acadia National Park

a lobsterman checks his traps. Find a spot tucked in a crag or the shade of a coastal pine for relaxed viewing as the summer sun burns away the fog and Schoodic Point looms through the mists across the mouth of Frenchman Bay. This straightforward coastal stroll can readily be extended into a satisfying half-day hike from a seaside strand to a granite mountain peak. For an adventurous return from Otter Point, just cross the road at the Gorham Mountain trailhead, climb to the mountaintop, and loop back to Sand Beach on the challenging Beehive route.

Two national-park campgrounds (Blackwoods and Seawall) are located on Mount Desert Island. Blackwoods is uniquely convenient and requires reservations, but except for terrific interpretive programs the sites aren't all that special. Access to the park's attractions is so convenient by car, however, that people can fully experience the beauty of Mount Desert Island by commuting from a comfortable lodge. Bar Harbor has swarms of hotels, motels, inns and restaurants that, of course, are always busy. For a quiet but active stay, find shelter in one of the smaller harbors that are surrounded by the park, and check out a selection of ranger programs and boat tours offering whale watches, puffin cruises, deep-sea fishing, windjammer sails, and excursions to the Cranberry Isles.

The practical guide

Access: Mount Desert Island, Bar Harbor, and Acadia National Park are southeast of Bangor at the end of Maine Highway 3. From the junction of U.S. Highways 1 and 1A with Maine Highway 3 in Ellsworth, follow Highways 1 North and 3 East 1.1 mile and then continue straight on 3 East where Highway 1 forks left. After 7.9 miles of gaudy tourist attractions, Highway 3 crosses a bridge onto Mount Desert Island and bears left 0.6 mile later toward the town of Bar Harbor. Measured from the bridge on Highway 3 that crosses onto Mount Desert Island, it's 18.3 miles to the Hulls Cove Entrance to Acadia National Park, the visitor center, and the start of the Park Loop Road, 21.5 miles to the town of Bar Harbor, and 27.0 miles to the entrance to the Blackwoods Campground.

For Southwest Harbor, Bass Harbor, Seawall Campground, and portions of Acadia National Park west of Somes Sound, bear right 0.6 mile beyond the Mount Desert Island bridge and follow Maine Highways 102 and 102A.

At first glance, the Park Loop Road that overlays the state highways and town roads seems to create a jumble, but the system is truly ingenious. You won't be trapped on a 20-mile drive that doesn't have an exit. Access points are convenient, and Cadillac Mountain, Otter Point, the Nature Center, entrances to carriage roads, and other highlights can be reached without driving the entire loop. A fee is collected only at the beginning of a one-way section just north of Sand Beach.

Accommodations and reservations: The Blackwoods Campground is open year-round. Reservations are required from mid-June to mid-September, and advised at other times. Make campground reservations through Destinet, 9450 Carroll Park Drive, San Diego, CA 92121, Tel. (800) 365-2267. Seawall Campground is open from May through September only, on a first-come first-served basis.

An extensive guide to accommodations and attractions is available from the Bar Harbor Chamber of Commerce at the address below. Most of the major national chains of motels and inns are represented on Mount Desert Island. The list below is only a sample of other options:

Bar Harbor: Acadia Hotel, 20 Mount Desert St., Bar Harbor, ME 04609, Tel. (207) 288-5721; Bar Harbor Hotel-Bluenose Inn, 90 Eden St., Bar Harbor, ME 04609, Tel. (800) 445-4077; Bar Harbor Inn, Newport Drive, Box 7, Bar Harbor, ME 04609, Tel. (800) 248-3351; Holbrook House, 74 Mount Desert St., Bar Harbor, ME 04609, Tel. (207) 288-4970; The Stratford House Inn, 45 Mount Desert St., Bar Harbor, ME 04609, Tel. (207) 288-5189.

Northeast Harbor: Asticou Inn, P.O. Box 406, Northeast Harbor, ME 04662, Tel. (800) 258-3373.

Southwest Harbor: The Inn at Southwest, Box 593, 371 Main Street, Southwest Harbor, ME 04679, Tel. (207) 244-3835

Maps: An informative brochure that includes a map of Mount Desert Island is available at the park's visitor and information centers. Additional information, trail maps, and guides to the carriage roads are also available upon request.

For further information: Acadia National Park, P.O. Box 177, Bar Harbor, ME 04609, Tel. (207) 288-3338; Bar Harbor Chamber of Commerce, 93 Cottage St., P.O. Box 158, Bar Harbor, ME 04609-0158, Tel. (207) 288-3393.

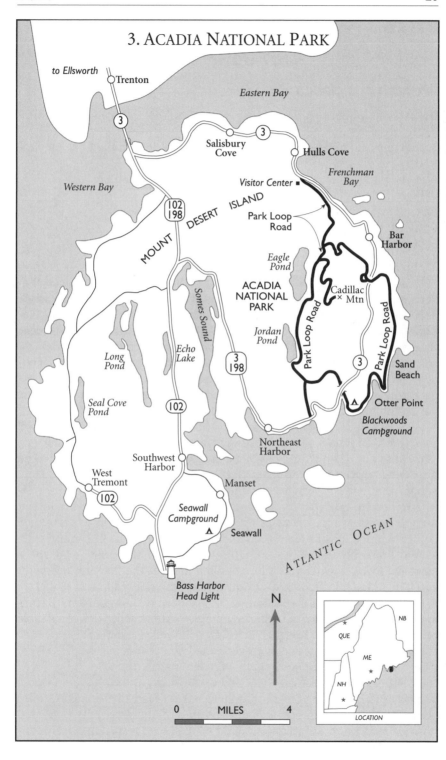

3. ACADIA NATIONAL PARK

to Ellsworth

Trenton

Eastern Bay

Western Bay

Salisbury Cove

Hulls Cove

Frenchman Bay

Visitor Center ■

Park Loop Road

MOUNT DESERT ISLAND

Bar Harbor

Eagle Pond

ACADIA NATIONAL PARK

Cadillac × Mtn

Park Loop Road

Somes Sound

Jordan Pond

Park Loop Road

Long Pond

Echo Lake

Sand Beach

Seal Cove Pond

Otter Point

Blackwoods Campground

Northeast Harbor

Southwest Harbor

West Tremont

Manset

Seawall Campground

Seawall

Bass Harbor Head Light

ATLANTIC OCEAN

N

0   MILES   4

QUE

NB

ME

NH

LOCATION

Maine

4. Loon Lodge and Allagash Lake
North Maine Woods

Allagash at a glance

Destination: Wilderness lodge and campsites in the forests of northern Maine

Location: North of Greenville and west of Millinocket, in the Allagash Wilderness Waterway

Access: Private gravel logging roads and a one-mile portage

Difficulty: Moderate

Accommodations: Rustic lodge and waterfront campsites

Duration: From two nights to an extended stay

Featured attractions: A wilderness lake and plentiful wildlife

A ribbon of lakes, ponds, and freshwater streams that courses more than 90 miles through the heart of the North Maine Woods, the Allagash Wilderness Waterway enjoys a reputation as a place for vigorous outdoor action. Established by the State of Maine in 1966 and protected as a National Wild and Scenic River as early as 1970, the Allagash Wilderness Waterway preserves an isolated corridor where the hazards, hardships, trials, and excitement of self-reliant travel can be experienced in the modern age. White water, remote locations, long distances, and limited access make the Allagash a destination for experienced campers and canoeists. It's not a place where you expect to spend an easy couple of days.

Set apart in a corner of this waterway system, Allagash Lake is well removed from routes that are usually traveled. No mechanized vehicle is allowed to approach within a mile of this pristine lake, no float plane, no four-wheel-drive truck, no motorized craft to negotiate tributaries. Most parties that enter Allagash Lake embark on long-distance journeys, putting in several miles to the west at Johnson Pond and planning to exit several miles east on a flowage into Chamberlain Lake. These traditional points of entry are fine for extended one-way adventures, but round trips to and from these sites require wrong-way travel on remote wilderness streams. In high water you'll be paddling against the flow. In low water you'll be lining a loaded canoe over miles of waterlogged gravel.

Happily, there is a solution to the Allagash access problem that allows competent paddlers a night of comfort at a rustic lodge before a simple one-mile walk leads to Allagash Lake. Only three special items are needed to assure this easy access: a high-clearance vehicle (not necessarily 4WD), a wheeled canoe caddy, and plenty of insect repellent.

Other camps in Maine may be harder to get to, but none are more remote than Loon Lodge. About 90 miles north of Greenville and 70 miles west of Millinocket, this self-sufficient outpost on the shore of Round Pond has no competition within a span of 60 miles. Given its isolation, a rough-cut rustic look should come as no surprise, and the black Lab and the tail-wagging hound that meet you by the road add to the hunting-camp aura. Still, after a long drive into this region, the three cabins above the pond can't help but look inviting. Wood stoves for heat, gas stoves for cooking, firm bunks, gas lights, and a bathhouse with toilets and hot showers make the cabins restful shelters. Add a main lodge with beamed ceiling, soft couches, a dining room serving hearty meals, and a view of Round Pond, and you've discovered a comfortable haven that acts as a staging ground for treks into Allagash Lake.

Remote corners of the north woods are no place for low-slung roadsters, but the average sport-utility or other high-clearance vehicle should have no trouble driving the

Leaving the Loon Lodge dining hall

2.4 miles from Loon Lodge to the Allagash Wilderness Waterway gate. If you have doubts about your vehicle, ask Mike, who runs the lodge, about charges for transport service. Otherwise, bear left as you leave the lodge and then turn right onto a narrow lane directly opposite the Round Pond North Campsite. Fork left as the lane divides in another mile and try to be nonchalant as you parallel a beaver dam on a road that dips below the level of the pond. Less than a mile of rough road ends at a locked metal gate where you'll also find space for parking exactly a mile from Allagash Lake.

A one-mile portage is rarely fun, but a wheeled canoe caddy makes this overland trek a snap. Following a discontinued driveway to a little-used ranger cabin, the even surface of a grassy lane rises up and over a low divide with only an occasional rock or hole to hinder easy progress. Ignore the rough carry trail that juts off to the right. Continue straight on the broad lane until it drops past the ranger cabin and ends in a large clearing at the elbow of an arm reaching out from Allagash Lake.

About four miles long and two miles wide, the main body of Allagash Lake is hidden from view while you stand in the cabin clearing. As you might discover later, though, the lake looks roughly rectangular when seen from above, with an inlet and an outlet attached at its northern corners and a bending arm that hooks to the south and west. Several campsites service canoe routes that cross from inlet to outlet, but three sites can also be found on the quieter southern shores, especially convenient to paddlers who portage in for a shorter stay. The Carry Trail camp-

site occupies a hidden cove around a point to the right of the cabin clearing, while the protected Island site lies three miles distant at the southeast corner of the lake. For an easy paddle to a convenient site that won't
leave you stranded in the brisk prevailing winds, consider instead the
Ede's site, across the arm from the cabin clearing. The brown-and-yellow
campsite sign is lost in a tangle of brush. Look for several yards of sandy
beach on the rim of the far shore for a clue to the site's location.

After resting awhile or setting up camp, it's time to get out on the
water and surround yourself with the pallet of green that circles this wilderness lake. Cedar, fir, spruce, and pine, moss, alder, fern, and reed
mingle along the shore in shades that defy description. Except in the southwest quadrant, where Allagash Mountain bumps into the sky, a low, flat
ripple of hills rings the leafy shore and contributes a measure of silence to
a hush that becomes enchanting. Without the hum of civilization, time on
Allagash Lake is marked by the sounds of nature. The haunting call of a
loon, the whir of feathers above a tent, or the resonant rap of a wood-
pecker take on added weight. Months later, memories of sounds may even
define your trip: the splash and drip of rhythmic paddles pulling across
the lake, the gurgling plop of a hungry fish roiling the evening water, or
the snort of a stag on a moonlit night in the glow of the northern lights.

On bright afternoons, the clearing near the ranger cabin draws canoes from all around the lake to a different outdoor attraction. For a great
change of pace, look to the edge of the woods just north of the ranger
cabin for a trail that climbs to a firetower on the top of Allagash Mountain.
The surprisingly hard ascent takes the better part of an hour, but the view
from the top is an excellent introduction to the entire Allagash region.
Even newcomers spot a list of distinctive features. Look for the rounded
mound of Mount Kineo high above Moosehead Lake, the prominent mass
of Mount Katahdin, Maine's highest peak, and the nearby shore of Round
Pond, where your journey to this summit started. Although most of neigh-

A popular landing near the base of Allagash Mountain

boring Chamberlain Lake is hidden by nearby hills, ponds and marshes dot the surrounding landscape, and Allagash Lake looms so large that even from the top of the tower, the sweep of its wild north-woods waters exceeds your field of vision.

The practical guide

Access: The only access to Allagash Lake is over privately owned timber roads. While it's possible to travel west from Millinocket, road conditions on that route are presently very poor. Take the Greenville approach, especially with family vehicles.

Most of the timber lands in northern Maine are now separated into two administrative units; the southern "West Branch Region" managed by Great Northern Paper and the northern unit of nearly 3 million acres managed by North Maine Woods, Inc., an organization of multiple owners. Travelers from Greenville to Round Pond or Allagash Lake will pass through both jurisdictions. Several essential points need to be kept in mind: entry and day-use fees are charged for admission to this private land, checkpoints are not open late at night, and logging trucks under all circumstances and without question are entitled to the right of way.

From exit 39 of Interstate 95, follow Maine Highway 7 15 miles north and turn left onto Maine Highway 23 in the town of Dexter. After 11 more miles turn left again onto Maine Highways 6 and 15 and continue north 28 miles to the town of Greenville. Except for the final outpost at Kokadjo, Greenville is your last chance for gasoline and supplies. Make sure that you leave the Greenville/Kokadjo area with a full tank and all your other needs.

From Greenville, drive in the direction of Lily Bay and Kokadjo on the highway that skirts the southeast side of Moosehead Lake. After 19 miles pass the Kokadjo store and continue ahead on a road that is now gravel. Keep right at the junction with the road to Spencer Camps and left at the road to Medawisa Camps (the road to the camps may be in better condition than the road you have to travel) and look for the Sias Hill, Bowater Great Northern checkpoint about 5 miles beyond Kokadjo. Tell the attendant that you're on the way to Loon Lodge and Allagash Lake. No fees are charged if you're merely passing through.

About 9 miles from the Sias Hill checkpoint, turn left at the T intersection with the Golden Road, cross the West Branch of the Penobscot River after 17 miles, and turn right on the unmarked Ragmuff Road 2 miles beyond the river crossing. Follow signs for Loon Lodge or the Caucomgomoc Checkpoint, which you reach after another 26 miles. You are now entering the North Maine Woods region and will pay the appropriate fee. In 1997, daily nonresident rates were $7 per person, $5 per night for camping, or a one-time fee of $21 for overnight sporting-camp visitors.

From the Caucomgomoc Checkpoint, continue straight through a four-way intersection and turn right after 4.7 miles, following signs to

Caucomgomoc Lake. Drive 6.4 more miles and turn left at a three-way junction at a large Loon Lodge sign. Continue around the shore of Round Pond, cross the inlet, pass the Round Pond North Campsite, and in 0.5 mile you'll find the long Loon Lodge driveway.

Accommodations and reservations: Campsites cannot be reserved in the Allagash Wilderness Waterway, including Allagash Lake, but campers who search for a spot in the early afternoon should have a choice of sites. Sites have picnic tables, fire rings, and pit toilets.

Guests at Loon Lodge can choose to cook their own meals or eat in the dining room. Bring any food you plan to prepare as well as towels, sheets, and blankets (or sleeping bags). Loon Lodge is not open in the winter months. For reservations and information from May 1 to November 30 contact Michael Yencha, P.O. Box 480, Millinocket, ME 04462, Tel. (207) 695-2821; from December 1 to April 30 contact Michael Yencha, P.O. Box 2469, Wilkes-Barre, PA 18703, Tel. (717) 287-6915

Maps: USGS Allagash Lake, Caucomgomoc Lake East, and Tramway quads. North Maine Woods Inc. and Great Northern Paper, Inc. publish very good maps of their respective regions. Maps are available for purchase at all checkpoints and from the addresses below.

For further information: Great Northern Paper, Inc., Public Relations, One Katahdin Ave., Millinocket, ME 04462-1398, Tel. (207) 723-5131, Ext. 1229; North Maine Woods, P.O. Box 421, Ashland, ME 04732, Tel. (207) 435-6213; Allagash Wilderness Waterway, Maine Bureau of Parks and Recreation, State House Station 22, Augusta, ME 04333, Tel. (207) 287-3821.

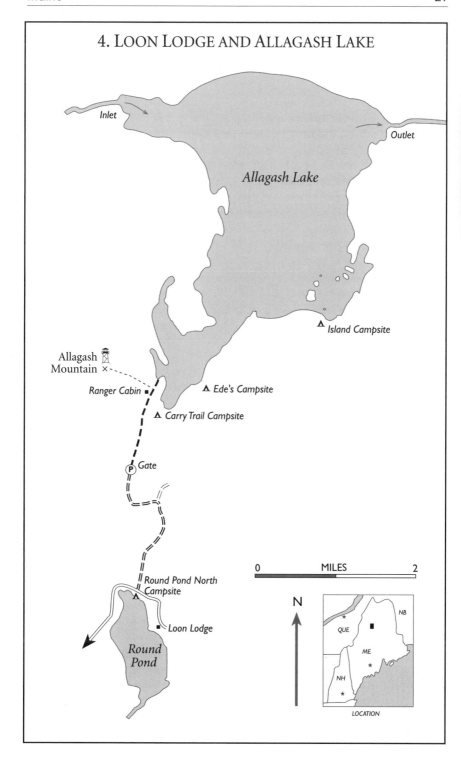

4. LOON LODGE AND ALLAGASH LAKE

Inlet

Outlet

Allagash Lake

△ Island Campsite

Allagash
Mountain ×
Ranger Cabin ■

△ Ede's Campsite

△ Carry Trail Campsite

Ⓟ Gate

Round Pond North
Campsite
△
■ Loon Lodge

*Round
Pond*

0   MILES   2

N

QUE   NB
             ME
NH

LOCATION

5. Chesuncook Lake House
Chesuncook Village, Maine

Chesuncook at a glance

Destination: Historic inn on a wilderness lake
Location: Northern Maine, about 50 miles northwest of Millinocket
Access: Canoe, water taxi, or float plane; not accessible by motor vehicle
Difficulty: Moderate by canoe, otherwise Easy
Accommodations: Comfortable lake-front inn
Duration: From two days to more than a week
Featured attractions: Wildlife, peaceful paths, and the history of Henry
   Thoreau

Henry David Thoreau may have lived the simple life at Walden Pond, but for real adventure even Thoreau favored the wilds of northern Maine. Modern travelers can still retrace the path of the famous naturalist who found his way to Chesuncook Lake twice in the 1850s, where he camped, traveled by canoe, and visited the homestead of Ansel Smith. Accommodations in Chesuncook Village have greatly improved since Thoreau's exploration, when Smith's crude lodgings catered to the needs of timber crews. Today, in its second century, the historic Chesuncook Lake House rests on the shore of the third largest lake in Maine, entertaining travelers with views of Mount Katahdin and miles of watery wilderness little scarred by the passing years.

   Nestled at the northern end of 19-mile Chesuncook Lake near the inlet of the West Branch of the Penobscot River, Chesuncook Village reposes in the charm of a long-past era, a remote hamlet disconnected from the rest of the world. The dirt track that links a few homes and scattered lodges with the public landing on Graveyard Point fades into conifers at the edge of town, a guarantee that the handful of residents won't soon be swallowed by tourist hordes. Wildlife and solitude are the stock and trade of this magical realm, where Bert and Maggie McBurnie have provided hearty meals with a French flair and all the comforts of home for nearly 40 years.

   The journey to Chesuncook Village can be easy and cheap, or as daring as your budget allows. For a vigorous trip that tracks a portion of Thoreau's expedition, depart Moosehead Lake at North East Carry on a multiple-day excursion down the West Branch of the Penobscot River, exploring Lobster Lake and Pine Stream before reaching the waiting inn. Less energetic travelers can rely on the McBurnies, who ferry guests 18 miles up Chesuncook Lake from a boat launch on the Golden Road, while those in a hurry can choose the expensive option, a door-to-door float-plane flight from Greenville on Moosehead Lake. Of course, each of these alternatives requires logistical support and a degree of prior planning. For independent types with paddling skills who like to go it alone, there is another option.

Traversing bays and narrows at the northern end of Chesuncook Lake, the back-door route from Umbazooksus Stream avoids the longest fetch on this slender slice of water, but make sure you're familiar with canoeing big lakes before committing to this trip. Freshening winds and white caps can wreak havoc with an open boat, and a mile-long crossing of a long lake can be scary in a small canoe. Still, between the put in on a gravel beach and the solitary landing at Chesuncook Village, travelers departing in calm winds and gentle chop can look forward to a six-mile

paddle through the heart of the wild north woods. Just keep an eye on the western sky and watch for loons that cry in flight, a sure sign of inclement weather.

When Joe Polis guided Henry Thoreau through this stretch of the Maine woods, the narrow thread of

Remote flowage off Umbazooksus Road

Umbazooksus Stream channeled their winding journey through meadows of wetland sedge edged by thickets of streamside willows. Backtracking Thoreau's early route 140 years later, travelers today launch their canoes into a current long since transformed into an arm of Chesuncook Lake. Widened and deepened by completion of the Ripogenous Dam early in the 20th century, a slender 2.5-mile bay now stretches southwest toward Gero Island at the head of Chesuncook Lake. Calm paddling near the lee shore of this narrow Umbazooksus arm passes close by boreal forests as hemlock, spruce, birch and fir crowd the wooded banks. Unseen in the wilderness landscape are remnants of the region's past, where boom logs once careened down forest streams and steam engines snaked through woods on iron tracks that still rust beneath the trees. Coasting along this placid shore, with droplets of lake sprinkling from a silent paddle, a new sense of space and distance acclimates visitors to northern Maine. A small splash across the water rivets your attention, while the echo of a chain saw miles away merely deepens the abiding stillness that hovers in the air.

Gliding through a slight constriction at the south end of Umbazooksus Stream, canoes point directly at Gero Island, a former peninsula now separated by a skinny channel from the mainland's eastern shore. Bear southwest across the 1.5-mile length of a roughly rectangular bay and keep Gero Island on your left. Loons provide entertainment in the sweep of these open waters, but geese and mergansers frolic close to shore as you hug the Gero coast and round through a narrow channel into the head of Chesuncook Lake.

Apprehension is normal as you enter these expansive waters. If blustery winds are to cause rough going, the worst will show up here. To the southeast, the body of the lake stretches 19 miles to the Golden Road, while off to your right the dead water of Caucomgomoc Stream backs 10 miles northwest through Black Pond to Caucomgomoc Lake, and the West Branch of the Penobscot arrives from North East Carry, completing a 20-mile leg. If the weather doesn't cooperate, just hole up on Gero Island until calmer winds and waves make it safe to cross. The landings of several campsites double as convenient rest stops along the western shore, and serve as alternate quarters for paddlers who like to rough it the traditional way.

Finding your destination isn't a problem if you stick close to Gero Island. Sooner or later, the white clapboards on Chesuncook Lake House shine like a beacon to guide you to the opposite shore. Paddling west across the lake, details of Chesuncook Village slowly blossom with your approach: the public landing on the jutting point, scattered lodges along the shore, the birch-lined path, an emerald lawn, lilacs and wooden chairs, and maybe even a hunting dog meandering down to meet you near the rainbow of upturned hulls that line a private dock.

The greeting inside the inn is equally reassuring. Hot coffee or a cool drink helps you settle in to a cozy room overlooking the majestic lake and sunrises over Mount Katahdin. Just don't expect some upscale lodge. Up to a dozen guests share the bathrooms at the top of the stairs, and well-mannered pointers and spaniels might loiter in the entry hall of an inn

Chesuncook Lake House

that pampers by wilderness standards. There's a wood stove in the parlor, Segovia on public radio, and one enormous table that holds magazines and tired feet in front of a comfortable couch. Old patterns of pressed tin line the whitewashed walls, and the lights stay on until 10:30 for anyone still awake after downing a meal of roast beef, homegrown vegetables, and desserts made with native berries.

Getting to Chesuncook Lake House is a grand adventure, but not the end of the backwoods fun. After a breakfast of blueberry pancakes and plenty of coffee, Maggie McBurnie will be happy to pack a traveling lunch to fuel a daily excursion into nearby terrain, while canoes and boats can be rented by those who didn't float here on their own. Paddle over for a hike on Gero Island or complete a circumnavigation looking for wildlife along the way. On long summer days, more ambitious canoeists might tackle an exploration that even Thoreau overlooked. Bear northwest into the deadwater of Caucomgomoc Stream as far as time allows, where moose, herons, loons, and ducks can be spotted along the shore. If brook trout, lake trout, or landlocked salmon happen to be your passion, throw a fly rod into your boat, and head up the mouth of the West Branch to the hot spots on Pine Stream.

On lazy days, a chair on the porch may be just what the doctor ordered, or you can walk in the woods that reach back from shore to spot wildflowers and woodland game. My favorite short excursion is a simple tour of the village. Follow the road that passes the shore and curls past a clapboard church. Footpaths branch west to a sun-splotched glade where Thoreau's host is buried, and east to the dock that serves as a public landing. Gazing into a freshening breeze, watching waves chop across miles of lake, it's a comfort to know a warm bed awaits while you're out here roughing it easy.

The practical guide

Access: To reach the put in at Umbazooksus Stream, depart Interstate 95 at exit 56, pass through Millinocket following signs toward Baxter State Park, and bear left about 22 miles west of the interstate highway through the gateway to the West Branch Region. Enter the private domain of Great Northern Paper at Debsconeag Checkpoint and pay the moderate fees that apply. Paper companies literally own these gravel roads. Keep a sharp lookout for logging trucks and yield the right-of-way.

From Debsconeag, drive 18.4 miles west on the Golden Road as it skirts the West Branch of the Penobscot River, and turn right over a green bridge onto Telos Road, a broad gravel highway that speeds your journey north. After 14.6 miles on Telos Road, you'll pass through the Telos Checkpoint and enter the region managed by North Maine Woods Inc. Pay applicable fees and tolls, and let the ranger know where you're planning to spend the night. Umbazooksus Road appears on the left 8.7 miles beyond the Telos gate at a broad intersection almost within sight of a ranger station on the Allagash Wilderness Waterway. Follow Umbazooksus Road 8.2 miles west to a bridge that crosses the end of an apparent lake, and turn left again after 0.9 mile into a campsite marked as Umbazooksus West. Plenty of parking and a driveway straight to the water make for a convenient launch from a gravel beach at the northeast end of Umbazooksus Stream. All roads on this trip are well marked and suitable for family cars.

To access prearranged pickup from the Golden Road at the south end of Chesuncook Lake, follow the directions above, but don't turn north onto Telos Road. Instead, continue west about four miles to the Maine Fire Service boat launch on the north side of the Golden Road.

Several outfitters in Greenville and Millinocket operate float-plane charters in the area. The largest is Folsom's Air Service in Greenville, Tel. (207) 695-2821.

Accommodations and reservations: Bert and Maggie McBurnie, Chesuncook Village, Rt. 76, Box 656, Greenville, ME 04441, Tel. (207) 745-5330 preferably between the hours of 8 PM and 10 PM daily. The Lake House is open May to October, but housekeeping cabins are open all year to accommodate winter sports enthusiasts. A rate sheet is available for shuttle service, boat rental, housekeeping cabins, and Lake House American Plan. Reservations and deposit are required.

Maps: Regional maps of logging roads are available at the various checkpoints from Great Northern Paper, Inc. and North Maine Woods, Inc.; See also the USGS Chesuncook quad.

For further information: Great Northern Paper, Public Relations, One Katahdin Ave., Millinocket, ME 04462-1398, Tel. (207) 723-5131, Ext. 1229; North Maine Woods, Inc., P.O. Box 421, Ashland, ME 04732, Tel. (207) 435-6213.

5. CHESUNCOOK LAKE

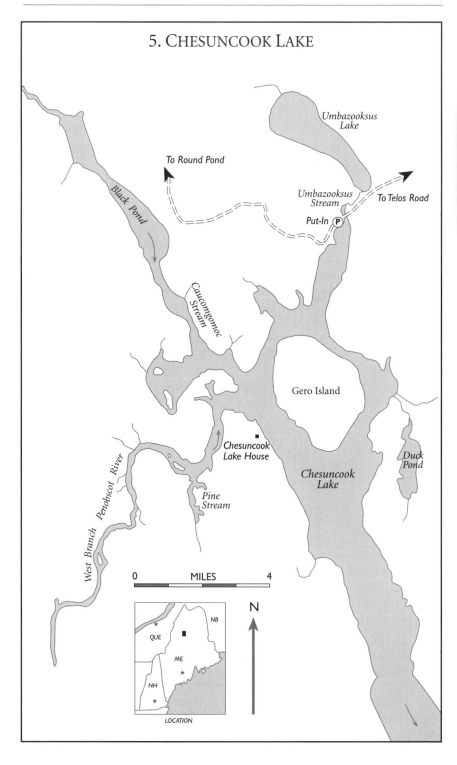

Umbazooksus
Lake

To Round Pond

Umbazooksus
Stream   To Telos Road

Put-In P

Black Pond

Caucomgomoc
Stream

Gero Island

Duck
Pond

Chesuncook
Lake House

Chesuncook
Lake

West Branch Penobscot River

Pine
Stream

0   MILES   4

N

NB

QUE

ME

NH

LOCATION

6. Cobscook Bay State Park
and
Moosehorn National Wildlife Refuge

Dennysville, Maine

Maine

Cobscook at a glance

Destination: A drive-in state park campground on the shore of Whiting
 Bay
Location: Down-east Maine, about 10 miles west of Lubec and Eastport
Access: Paved and gravel roads to campsites
Difficulty: Easy
Accommodations: Spacious waterfront sites
Duration: From 2 to 14 nights
Featured attractions: Moose, eagles, osprey, seals, whales, clams, and ter-
 rific family camping

Part of the Moosehorn National Wildlife Refuge in extreme down-east Maine,
Cobscook Bay State Park is not your typical public campground. Connected by a maze of inlets and coves to Cobscook Bay, Passamaquoddy
Bay, and finally the Atlantic Ocean, its spacious waterfront sites give campers a firsthand look at the region's 21-foot tides as well as a perfect chance
to gather a seaside dinner. Along with the privilege of camping on the
shore of this remarkable estuary is the right to collect clams. Bring a
bucket and fork onto the muddy flats of Whiting Bay that beckon at low
tide and help yourself to a peck of mollusks for each person in your party.
Best of all, in spite of the scenery and free food, there's virtually no one
here. Except on midsummer weekends, campers have a choice of sites on
wooded points or in hidden coves, with the wilds of Maine within easy
reach a short drive or paddle away.

Family recreation is a specialty at Cobscook Bay. Most campsites
are large and unusually private, and border shallow water. A number of
camps come equipped with wood-roofed picnic tables, while some even
offer the comfort and protection of sturdy Adirondack shelters. Walk-in
sites and tent sites are well removed from mobile units, and the large
lawn of the play area is separate from the sleeping quarters. A boat ramp,
a nature trail, hot showers, and down-east views from a hilltop firetower
round out the park's attractions. All in all, it's a terrific family base camp
for exploring the Moosehorn refuge or venturing among the islands and
inlets of secluded Cobscook Bay.

Black lines on red rock mark the levels of the highest tides in this
section of down-east Maine, while vast acres of tide pools, rock weed, and
clam flats are exposed by the ebbing sea. The horizontal distance between
the high and low water marks far exceeds the vertical change in the depth

of Cobscook Bay. Depending on the time of day, your tent may be 30 yards from the edge of the salty water or nearly a quarter mile away. Investigating the broad expanse of this tidal zone is a favorite pastime of younger campers, while canoes and kayaks are popular with adults in spite of the currents and tides. In a rising tide or a slack tide, launch a boat from your campsite into the mists of early morning or the quiet evening gloam. Osprey, seals, and the startling beauty of the rocky coast contribute serene pleasures to these flat inland waters, which rise with a rapid surge but lack the danger of crashing surf. Obtain the appropriate NOAA chart and use extreme caution, however, if you venture out of Whiting Bay. A "reversing falls" and other hazards wait at narrow passes between bays at every change of tide.

For land-based exploration, the Moosehorn National Wildlife Refuge offers more than 24,000 acres, many of which are included within designated wilderness areas. A center for research and management of the declining American woodcock, Moosehorn provides breeding habitat for migratory waterfowl and a permanent home for watchable mammals like black bear, moose, and white-tailed deer. Most visitors, though, focus their attention on the bald eagles that can often be found nesting in either section of the two-part Moosehorn Refuge. Check the tidal wetlands in the Edmunds unit, which holds the state park or the man-made platforms that rise within sight of US Highway 1 about 25 miles north of the campground in the larger Baring unit.

Over 50 miles of roads and trails course through the rolling hills of maple, birch, spruce, and fir that compose the Moosehorn Refuge. Abutting the state park campground on the opposite side of Highway 1, a 3.8-mile loop on South Trail, Crane Mill Road, and North Trail gives drivers

Waterfront campsite, Cobscook Bay State Park

an easy chance to locate wildlife as they creep through the woods and pass marshes at Hallowell Flowage. Hikers and bikers, though, are better off beginning their Moosehorn visit at the headquarters in the Baring Unit. Three nature trails and a chance to observe woodcock-banding operations especially appeal to birders, while anyone will enjoy walking or biking a convenient 2.7-mile loop past streams, ponds, and wetland marshes at the edge of a wilderness zone. Throughout the refuge, gravel roads that are closed to vehicles touch lakes and streams where fishing is permitted, and do-it-yourselfers are invited to bushwack to hidden ponds in the heart of a forest without trails.

When you leave the refuge headquarters, head north on Charlotte Road. Within 3.5 miles you'll pass a handicap-accessible fishing platform on a marshy branch of the Magurrewock River before arriving at a deck for observing osprey and bald eagles just across Highway 1. Remember to bring binoculars. As signs make very clear, it is absolutely forbidden to intrude on the territory of these magnificent nesting birds.

Binoculars also help at a final destination. Having driven this far you won't want to miss the peninsula of West Quoddy Head, the easternmost point in the United States and a glorious visual treat. Site of Quoddy Head State Park and a candy-striped red-and-white light, this rugged headland looks out to the frigid waters at the open end of the Bay of Fundy with foggy views of Canada's Campobello and Grand Manan islands. Walk down steps to the stony beach, clamber along the strand, feel seaweed beneath your feet, and engage all of your senses. Especially in August, you might be lucky enough to hear, see, and — some say — smell the breath of giant mammals as finback, humpback, minke, and right whales pass in their annual migrations.

The practical guide

Access: The entrance to Cobscook Bay State Park is 0.5 mile east of U.S. Highway 1 between Whiting and Dennysville, Maine. Turn east off

Canoeing in Whiting Bay

U.S. 1 onto Lower Edmunds Road at the state park sign 4.3 miles north of the junction of U.S. 1 and Maine Highway 189 (in Whiting) or 5.2 miles south of the junction of U.S. 1 and Maine Highway 86 (in Dennysville).

To reach the headquarters of the Moosehorn National Wildlife Refuge in the Baring Unit, drive north on U.S. Highway 1, pass the intersection with Highway 86 in Dennysville, and turn left onto Maine Highway 214 about 10 miles from Cobscook Bay State Park. Follow Highway 214 west 6.1 miles and turn right onto Charlotte Road. The entrance to the refuge headquarters is on the left, 8.5 miles north on Charlotte Road.

Access to the South Trail in the Edmunds Unit of the Moosehorn National Wildlife Refuge is on the west side of U.S. Highway 1, 0.2 mile south of the turn to Cobscook Bay State Park.

To find Quoddy Head State Park, drive east on Maine Highway 189 from Whiting. Signs for Quoddy Head will direct you to a right turn as you approach the town of Lubec.

Accommodations and reservations: Reservations at Cobscook Bay State Park can be made by mail, phone, fax, or in person, but forms must be completed and all fees paid at least 7 days prior to arrival. Although there are often vacancies, reservations allow you to select a particular site with the amenities you prefer. Contact the Maine Bureau of Parks and Lands at the address below.

The Moosehorn National Wildlife Refuge is open only from dawn to dusk. Office hours at refuge headquarters are weekdays from 7:30 AM. to 4:00 PM. A self-service information kiosk is open after hours.

Maps: For Cobscook Bay, National Oceanic and Atmospheric Administration (NOAA) chart #13328; Maps of the Moosehorn National Wildlife Refuge are available at refuge headquarters.

For further information: For Cobscook Bay State Park: Department of Conservation, Bureau of Parks and Lands, 22 State House Station, Augusta, ME 04333-0022, Tel. (207) 287-3824.

For Moosehorn National Wildlife Refuge, RR1, Box 202, Suite 1, Baring, ME 04694-9703, Tel. (207) 454-7161.

7. Daicey Pond

Baxter State Park, Maine

Maine

Daicey Pond at a glance

Destination: Pond-side cabins with views of Mount Katahdin
Location: North-central Maine, 18 miles west of Millinocket
Access: Gravel roads to the park and pond
Difficulty: Easy
Accommodations: Comfortable wilderness cabins
Duration: From overnight to two weeks
Featured attractions: Mountains, streams, lakes, and forests in the wild
  heart of Maine

Percival Baxter was a man of vision. A former governor with a dream of preserving the streams and forests that surround Mount Katahdin, Baxter made it his life's work to purchase more than 200,000 acres and give them to the State of Maine. The grant that became Baxter State Park may have seemed a bit eccentric in the early 1930s when most of the state already served as wild timberland. But at the end of the 20th century, as the pressures of logging and recreation take their toll on the northern forests, the gift of Percival Baxter becomes more precious every day.

The irony, of course, is that careful regulation is sometimes needed to insure wilderness freedom. Baxter intended this park to serve not only as a resource for outdoor recreation but also as a sanctuary that would stay forever wild. His wishes are strictly enforced. Unlike in many other state and national parks, snack bars, concession stands, and interpretive centers have never been part of the plan. Television sets, radios, and cellular phones cannot be used in the park. Pets aren't welcome, water spigots have been removed, and if you arrive with more people in your vehicle than stated in your reservation, you simply won't get in.

If the rules seem too restrictive, just remember what they prevent. Throngs of campers, the whine of chain saws, and disruption of the natural order are excluded from this park. What you'll find instead are the traditional pleasures that are part of wilderness Maine. Hunt, fish, and backpack, canoe a woodland lake, hike the hazardous Knife Edge Trail to the highest peak in the state, or just sit on the porch of a rustic cabin overlooking Daicey Pond as the sun sets on Mount Katahdin and swallows learn to fly.

Except for climbers trying to bag Mount Katahdin and through-hikers ending their journey on the Appalachian Trail, Baxter is not a park that visitors can "do" in a day or two. No geysers, scenic overlooks, or must-see natural features lend themselves to a "been there, done that" review. Instead, the mountains, streams, lakes and forests of Baxter State Park create a perfect setting to immerse yourself in nature and leisurely soak up a sense of a wild environment. To slow down, settle in, and experience Baxter in true comfort, there's no better spot than a primitive cabin at beautiful Daicey Pond.

On a gravel road less than 12 miles from the main entrance to Baxter State Park, Daicey Pond lies close to Nesowadnehunk Stream, about midway between the base of Mount Katahdin and the churning white-water rapids of the famous West Branch of the Penobscot River. Deep in the forest, nudging the final link in the Appalachian Trail, Daicey Pond is large enough to house nesting loons and to clear a stunning vista of Baxter's prominent peaks. Ringing the western shore, eleven log cabins take full advantage of their location, with extraordinary views of Katahdin's southwest flank reflecting in the placid pool.

Nesowadnehunk Stream, Baxter State Park

Neatly painted brown with green trim and red-floral curtains, the "wilderness" cabins at Daicey Pond are among the most comfortable you'll ever find. Outfitted with beds, woodstoves, gaslights, and chairs, these very roomy, well-maintained cabins appeal to guests who return year after year to rekindle their love of the north woods and renew summer friendships. With a handy dock that doubles as a canoe launch and a popular swimming hole, Daicey Pond also offers a special family appeal. On rainy days, a collection of vintage books and an assortment of jigsaw puzzles entertain young and old in the spacious log-cabin library, while rocking chairs on the shady porch share picture-perfect views of the towering mountain that rises across the water and a nest of tolerant swallows that live beneath the eaves.

In spite of its uncommon comfort, amenities are limited at Daicey Pond. Like camping in a cozy cabin, bring food, utensils, pots and pans, blankets, sheets (or sleeping bags), pillows, towels, a wash basin, and a bucket for carrying water from the pond. Fire rings, dry wood, and a splitting maul are provided for cooking over open flames, but most people bring a backpacking or a portable stove for use on the sheltered porch. Flashlights are handy for finding the outhouses that are scattered throughout the camps. When in doubt, bring everything you think you might possibly need. Extras can always be left inside your nearby car, but the 20-mile jaunt to Millinocket to obtain forgotten items takes at least three

Maine

or four hours round trip.

Once settled into your cabin, the immediate environs of Daicey Pond provide plenty of outdoor action. For a rigorous hike, the 7-mile trek on the Grassy Pond and Hunt trails to the top of Baxter Peak offers a very ambitious challenge. Be aware of Katahdin's reputation for hazardous, changeable weather, and remember that rangers can close trails in the event of adverse conditions. More moderate hikes also lie within reach of the Daicey cabins. Try the routes to Doubletop or Sentinel Mountain for peaks with views of Katahdin, explore an angler's path that follows Slaughter Brook, or find a trail that discovers the nearby shore of Lost Pond. Easy destinations can even be found along the Appalachian Trail, which leads south from Daicey Pond. Hike 0.9 mile to a house-sized chunk of granite below a washed-out dam where Little Niagara Falls provides mountain and white-water views, or continue an additional 0.3 mile to see the torrent of Nesowadnehunk Stream as it plunges over the impressive drop of Big Niagara Falls.

Surrounded by enticing trails, modest pleasures still seem to excel at Daicey Pond. Rent a canoe at the library dock and paddle from shore to shore, or pick up a printed guide at the Ranger cabin and follow a nature trail through the woods around the pond. For an evening's entertainment, become an observer of wildlife that roams throughout the park. Simply walk down the driveway and check out the local marsh, where a moose engrossed in a dusky dinner may create a counterpoint to the glow of the setting sun on the summit of Baxter Peak.

Daicey Pond, Mount Katahdin, and the view from the library dock

The primary access road within Baxter State Park does its part to enforce a laid-back approach to excursions beyond Daicey Pond. Not lightly does anyone tackle the 41.1 mile Perimeter Road that forms a letter "C" as it runs from Togue Pond Gate in the south, along the western boundary of the park, to the Matagammon Gatehouse high in the northeast corner. Twisting, narrow, and very rough, the condition of the Perimeter Road (also known as the Tote Road) barely accommodates family vehicles and certainly limits cruising. This is one place where a 20-mph speed limit can often be excessive, especially in the early evenings when moose and bear are apt to jump into the right of way. Count on at least five hours, excluding stops, if you feel the need to complete a round trip.

On the other hand, short drives (or mountain-bike rides) along the Perimeter Road bring campers at Daicey Pond to new attractions. In the 6.5-mile stretch from Foster Field near Daicey Pond to the open meadows of Nesowadnehunk Field, the Perimeter Road climbs and dives through constantly changing environs. Marshes, mountains, evergreen forests, and hardwood stands line the slender road as it passes trailheads to lesser summits and parallels a rushing river where fly-fishing anglers hook their limit and campers catch sight of balding peaks high above the stream. On a hot summer day, head south on the Tote Road for a swim at Abol Beach, or travel nearly 4 miles north to exciting Ledge Falls. Swirling water and polished rock at this popular roadside rest give sunbathers and intrepid swimmers an exhilarating chance to cap their day in the wild cascades of chilling Nesowadnehunk Stream.

The practical guide

Access: From Exit 56 of Interstate 95, follow Maine Highways 11 south and 157 west through East Millinocket to Millinocket. Baxter State Park signs will guide you west from Millinocket. About 22 miles west of the interstate, do not turn left through the Debsconeag Gate to the West Branch Region, but continue straight instead on the paved access road that leads to the Togue Pond Gatehouse in Baxter State Park.

Accommodations and reservations: Daicey Pond has limited capacity and is popular with local residents. The warm-weather season runs from mid-May to mid-October. Winter dates are available for snowmobile and ski access only. Reservations can be made beginning January 2 each year, but are not taken over the phone. Call for availability of particular dates, but reservations can be made only in person or by mail. Prime weeks and weekends in late July and August will generally be taken by early January. Unless you can show up at the park headquarters in Millinocket, obtain reservation forms in advance and mail your request as soon as you possibly can (right after Christmas if you're timing your visit for the height of the summer season).

Maps: A variety of Baxter State Park maps are available at the visitor center outside the Togue Pond Gate, at park headquarters in Millinocket, and at campgrounds within the park.

For further information: Baxter State Park, 64 Balsam Drive, Millinocket, ME 04462, Tel. (207) 723-5140.

8. Monhegan Village
Monhegan Island, Maine

Monhegan at a glance

Destination: Inn, rental home, or guest house 10 miles out to sea
Location: Between Bath and Rockland, Maine, at the mouth of Muscongus
   Bay
Access: Passenger ferry only, no vehicles on the island
Difficulty: Easy to Moderate
Accommodations: Comfortable rooms in classic inns or village homes
Duration: Day-trip, overnight, or extended summer stay
Featured attractions: Sea birds, seals, and ocean views from soaring head-
   land cliffs

If you love to watch harbor seals, you'll know the attraction of Monhegan Island. Not only will you find these creatures loafing in the sun, snoozing on sea-splashed rocks, and stirring themselves for dinner. After adjusting to island time, you'll very likely mimic their behavior.

Barely more than one square mile of mountaintop, 10 miles out to sea, easygoing Monhegan Island means different things to different people. It's a working harbor for fishing families who make it their year-round home, a haven for artists who lure customers on busy summer weekends, and a pleasant retreat for long-term guests just trying to get away. For bird watchers and outdoor folks, Monhegan offers plenty too. More than 17 miles of walking trails circle and cross the island, leading to pebble beaches, soaring cliffs, and wave-crashed ocean coves. Amidst the stunning scenery, hikers sooner or later find the time to loiter along the shore, enjoy a sunny lunch, or stare at the earth's horizon. Just like harbor seals.

There are no cars on Monhegan Island. There are, however, eight or ten pickup trucks in various stages of dilapidation that carry baggage from the wharf to your island home. Passengers arrive among lobster boats bobbing in the harbor and walk along dusty village roads to reach their accommodations. Look for the Island Inn above the harbor about 70 yards uphill, the Monhegan House a quarter mile distant at the south end of town, or any of several guest houses and rental homes sprinkled throughout the village.

Traffic consists of a golf cart, a kid on a bike, and a group of fellow strollers. Ambling between the general store, the fish market, and the bakery the people of Monhegan make main street the central social scene. Chance meetings and casual talks thrive in the easy rhythm of this gray-shingled town as visitors peruse craft shops, art galleries, and choice places to eat. If you're looking for something to do, check the down-east version of a web site on the side of a main-street shed, where restaurant menus,

The Island Inn, Monhegan Island, Maine

gallery schedules, puffin cruises, and times for guided walks are posted for the passing crowd.

Trails on the island are never hard to find. Walk out of the village in any direction and the gravel lane you are following soon dwindles to a trail. If you need to know where you're going, a local land trust publishes a handy map that's widely available from hotels and businesses on the island. Just heed the warning that the map isn't drawn to scale, and that intervals shown between trail junctions don't always portray the real distance involved.

The whole of Monhegan Island tilts slightly downward from north to south as well as from east to west. The highest headlands are therefore found in Monhegan's northeast quadrant while the village is logically located on the more hospitable southwest coast. For all of the easy walking you'll find on this slanting piece of rock, don't think that its limited size implies that its trails are always tame. Especially near the highest cliffs, rough and rocky paths often require footwear more substantial than worn in town. Keep in mind too that no hospital or firehouse exists on Monhegan Island. Because of its isolation, scarcity of water, and consequent fire hazard, hikers are not permitted to smoke outside the village.

Except for the cry of a herring gull and the clang of a distant buoy, the Blackhead Trail could be confused with any path through New England woods. A discreet sign marks a lane bearing northeast out of the village where the Blackhead Trail departs for granite headlands that confront the breaking surf. Passing over the crest of the island through a spruce and hemlock forest, one of the island's most difficult routes encounters wetland ferns, hairy sedge, and occasional blue flag iris, before scrambling to a ledge between Squeaker Cove and the top of Blackhead cliff. Labelled with green-and-white numbered signs that correspond to numbers on the locally published map, trails branch north and south from Blackhead's cross-island route. Scramble along the Cliff Trail (trail #1), which traces the craggy shore, or turn instead onto an easy-walking inland path that leads to the tip of the island. Bayberry and brambles give way to beach peas and the smell of the sea as trails #15 and #17 arrive at the northern shore. At slack tide, explore salty pools on Pebble Beach and look for lazy wildlife lounging on Seal Ledges before rejoining trail #1 that circles back to the north end of town past stony coves on the island's western shore.

An easier path to ocean views begins my favorite Monhegan tour, a two-hour loop from the middle of town to the magnificent Whitehead cliffs. Between the schoolhouse and the village library, turn east on a lane marked with a Whitehead sign. Climb past lawns sprinkled with roses to a sweeping panorama of the white-trimmed village across from Smutty Nose and Manana, the tiny islands that enclose Monhegan's harbor. Pause at Monhegan Light at the top of the hill with its local history museum, then continue east on a broad lane that narrows to a path as it briefly rises through stunted trees and ends on Whitehead's cliff. From Blackhead to the north to Burnthead to the south, the bulk of Monhegan's eastern shore meets the Atlantic Ocean within sight of this stunning point. As gulls swoop below your feet and perch on rocky ledges, you can while away an afternoon or greet the start of a brand new day.

After ogling the views and the soaring gulls, turn south on a portion of the Cliff Trail (trail #1) that plunges from Whitehead's top to rocks, waves, and thunderous sounds that gather in Gull Cove. Dodging the splash of breaking waves on the jumbled rock-bound shore, you'll likely find an artist or two tucked among the stones, sketching the shapes of the seaside world or seeking inspiration. Continue parallel to the rugged coast past bayberry, grass, and the bleached remains of beachfront trees as the trail climbs south again to the crown of Burnthead. Secluded outcrops pepper this cliff with nooks for ocean viewing before the Underhill Trail (trail #3) turns west near a firebox just beyond the top. A gentle meander through a highland meadow leads to the

Quiet moments at Monhegan Harbor

south end of town, where a right turn onto Lobster Cove Road returns you to the village.

Wherever you wander on Monhegan Island, be sure to be back by sunset to enjoy the evening show. From lighthouse hill and an overlook just opposite the village school, regulars gather to watch the glow of the sun as it drops below the coast of Maine. In the fading light just before dark herring gulls mass above the harbor. Gliding, swooping, and riding invisible currents of evening air, the gathering flock hovers over the wharf and dock-side houses until secret signals lead them to roost on the rocks of Smutty Nose Island.

The practical guide

Access: Passage to Monhegan Island is by passenger ferry only. Service is available from three locations, all of which can be reached via state highways that run south from U.S. Highway 1 between Wiscasset and Rockland, Maine.

From Boothbay Harbor (Maine Highway 27) The Balmy Days III, Boothbay Harbor, ME 04538, Tel. (800) 298-2284 (seasonal).

From New Harbor (Maine Highways 129 to 130) The Hardy Boat, P.O. Box 326, New Harbor, ME 04554, Tel. (800) 278-3346 (seasonal).

From Port Clyde (Maine Highway 131) Monhegan Boat Line, P.O. Box 238, Port Clyde, ME 04855, Tel. (207) 372-8848 (year-round).

Schedules vary from boat to boat and from season to season. Call ahead for reservations. Depending on point of departure, crossings last about 1 to 1 1/2 hours.

Accommodations and reservations: Island accommodations are limited and reservations are necessary, especially at the height of the summer season. Some cottages, rooms, and housekeeping units are available year-round, but the larger hotels and restaurants are closed from late October to early May. Rooms are comfortable and cuisine is excellent, but shared baths and informality are the general rule.

For an overnight or a week or more, try any of the following: The Island Inn, Box 128, Monhegan Island, ME 04852, Tel. (207) 596-0371; Monhegan House, Monhegan, ME 04852, Tel. (800) 599-7983; The Hitchcock House, Monhegan, ME 04852, Tel. (207) 594-8137; Shining Sails, P.O. Box 346, Monhegan Island, ME 04852, Tel. (207) 596-0041; The Trailing Yew, Monhegan, ME 04852, Tel. (207) 596-0440; The Tribler Cottage, Monhegan, ME 04852, Tel. (207) 594-2445.

Maps: Maps of the walking trails on Monhegan Island are available at ferry ticket counters on the mainland and at hotels and numerous businesses throughout Monhegan village.

For further information: For a guide to long-term house and cottage rentals, Shining Sails Rentals, P.O. Box 346, Monhegan Island, ME 04852, Tel. (207) 596-0041.

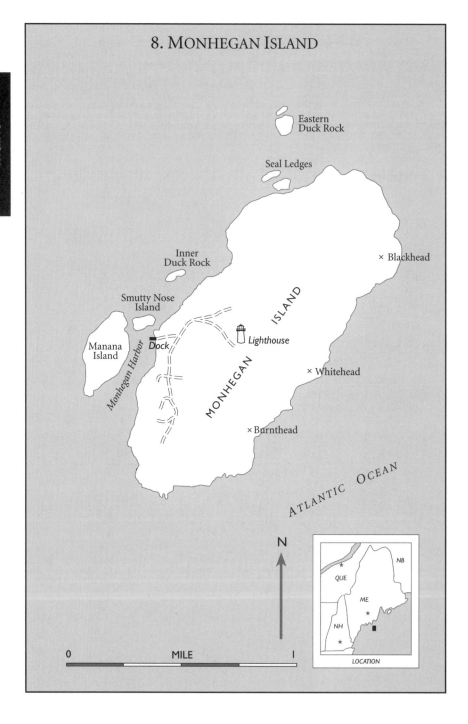

8. MONHEGAN ISLAND

Eastern
Duck Rock

Seal Ledges

Inner
Duck Rock

× Blackhead

Smutty Nose
Island

ISLAND

Lighthouse

Manana
Island

Dock

MONHEGAN

× Whitehead

Monhegan Harbor

× Burnthead

ATLANTIC OCEAN

N

QUE

NB

ME

NH

LOCATION

0   MILE   1

Maine

9. Sheepscot and Quahog Bays
Georgetown and Brunswick, Maine

Georgetown at a glance

Destination: Sea kayak getaways on the mid-coast of Maine
Location: South of Bath and Brunswick near Georgetown and Cundy's Harbor
Access: Paved roads to boat launches and inns
Difficulty: Moderate
Accommodations: Gracious Victorian inn or cozy bed and breakfast
Duration: Overnight or extended stay
Featured attractions: Ospreys, seals, unspoiled coasts, and the harbors of down-east Maine

Sea kayaking is not a sport you start on a casual basis. Waves, tides, paddling techniques, and thoughts of chilling self-rescue combine with issues of liability to prevent people from renting a kayak and learning on their own. If you're into this sport, you're into it all the way. Either you take lessons, buy a kayak, and venture out on your own, or you'll be content to stick with a group and paddle with a guide. Experienced kayakers also balk at revealing their favorite places. Getting a lead on a waterfront inn that's convenient to a worthy coast is somewhat akin to stealing trade secrets. To find a remote, comfortable site attractive to both experienced hands and beginners with a guide is really quite a feat.

Even landlubbers scanning a map will be drawn to the coast of Maine. From Cape Elizabeth to Quoddy Head fingers of earth that were scraped by glaciers point south toward the open sea, forming windy gulfs and protected bays laced with countless islands. Ospreys nest near these ragged coasts, seals inhabit the waters, and untold lobsters on the ocean bottom are the fishermen's favorite catch. Saltwater sailors have long plied these heavily travelled shores, but kayakers come face to face with a set of magnified problems. High tides, swift currents, frequent fogs, frigid seas, and unpredictable weather make inn-to-inn kayaking hard to plan even in the warmth of summer. The best bet is to find an inn within easy reach of the sea, where unspoiled shores, unpeopled islands, and close contact with nature will keep kayakers happily paddling for at least several days.

Centered near working harbors that survive by catching lobsters, two establishments on the southern mid-coast of Maine overlook terrific kayaking waters, yet avoid the heavy influence of the upscale yachting scene. To paddle out of these down-east ports is to experience life in Maine, where real people earn their living off a truly unspoiled coast and where paddlers are made to feel welcome. From either location, you can launch a kayak within sight of your inn's front door, or arrange for local guides to furnish a kayak, provide instruction, and paddle by your side as you cruise the rockbound coast.

Grey Havens Inn: High on a bluff above Sheepscot Bay, this superb Victorian inn built in 1904 has proudly earned a listing in the National Register of Historic Places. Flanked by three-story turrets containing rooms with sweeping views, the exterior of this classic shingle-style inn is defined by a wraparound porch where rocking chairs look out to sea beneath hanging pots of flowers. Brass beds, brass lamps, and narrow wood plank walls lend a proper nautical air to the interior of the inn, while high ceilings, hanging baskets, writing desks, and bookcases lining the upper halls convey a sense of sophistication.

To launch a seagoing kayak, walk down the bluff on a zigzag path that leads from the porch to a deep-water dock, or take a short drive to a stony beach near the Five Islands lobster hut. Either option puts kayakers on the western shore of the Sheepscot River as it enters Sheepscot Bay. From either put-in, hug the coast past Malden Island, head north to Goose Rock Passage, and enter Knubble Bay. Tidewater cruisers have several options in these intricate inland waters. From the end of Goose Rock Passage, turn south to Robinhood Cove, paddle a loop through Knubble Bay, or continue north to Beal Island, where the Appalachian Mountain Club maintains a campground and an easy perimeter trail. Beyond the tidal rips that flank Beal Island is the entrance to Hockomock Bay. Sprinkled with islands and surrounded by forests, this beautiful inland bay is a sheltered playground for kayaks, and about as far north as round-trip paddlers will venture in a day.

If tides and currents allow, kayakers might paddle an alternate course from the dock of the Grey Havens Inn across the mouth of the Sheepscot River. Check for seals and ospreys near Spring and Boston islands before looping back to Five Islands via Ebencook Harbor and Dogfish Head. If

Grey Havens Inn, overlooking Sheepscot Bay

you have the time, take a break on Whitman Island. Known locally as a "MITA" island, Whitman is a stop on a long-distance waterway maintained by the Maine Island Trail Association. The waterway is meant for hearty campers prepared for rough conditions, but you're welcome to stop and enjoy their islands as long as you leave no trace.

For a change of pace from paddling, drive two miles south from the Grey Havens Inn to Reid State Park. Picnic tables, pine trees, and beautiful rocky coves make fine spots to fire up a charcoal grill, especially after a day of lounging on a dune-backed sandy beach. From Todd's Point or Griffith's Head, visitors to this day-use park can walk the sandy strand, surf-cast in the Gulf of Maine, or simply fly a kite.

Bethel Point Bed & Breakfast: Rather than the grandeur of the Grey Havens Inn, paddlers might prefer the charm of Bethel Point. Quiet and unobtrusive, this cozy accommodation is the last house on an undiscovered coast, adjacent to a small boat ramp and a working lobster dock. Rooms with a shared bath and a separate suite with woodstove and kitchen both enjoy a view of a tiny cove where kayaks come and go just across a private lawn.

The protected waters of Quahog Bay and Ridley Cove match the character of the lodgings. Not exposed to a broad expanse like vast Sheepscot Bay, paddlers off Bethel Point are shielded from ocean swells by the bulk of Yarmouth Island. Setting out from the tiny cove after breakfast at Bethel Point, kayakers steer north past a cluster of small islands as they start a mellow voyage to the top of Quahog Bay. Consult your chart to find your way to Raspberry and Snow islands (both MITA stops) or enter a long dead-end channel that narrows to the intimate beauty of tranquil Card Cove.

For an alternate exploration, swing south and then east as you leave the bed and breakfast, round Bethel Point, stop for a picnic on Yarmouth Island, and cross Ridley Cove. You're approaching Cundy's Harbor, with its active lobster fleet sheltered by a narrow finger of land that expands to Cundy's Point. As long as you're here, cruise the circumference of Big Hen Island, where you might even spy what's left of a sunken shipwreck if you catch a very low tide.

H2Outfitters provides group lessons for beginning and intermediate paddlers, private lessons, a variety of packaged trips for beginning to expert kayakers, and private guide service. Within reasonable driving distance of both the Grey Havens Inn and the Bethel Point Bed & Breakfast, the people

Coastal cruising in a saltwater cove

at H2Outfitters are generous with advice and happy to meet your needs throughout the mid-coast region. If you're not an experienced kayaker, don't venture onto these waters without taking adequate lessons or being accompanied by a skilled kayak guide.

The practical guide

Access: Located on separate fingers of land, Grey Havens and Bethel Point are only 8 miles apart but divided by many more miles of highway driving.

To reach Grey Havens Inn, follow U.S. Highway 1 in Bath to the east end of the Carleton Bridge across the Kennebec River. Turn south onto Maine Highway 127, pass through the village of Georgetown, and 10.5 miles from Highway 1 bear right onto Seguinland Road. Grey Havens Inn is on your left after another 0.5 mile.

To reach Bethel Point Bed & Breakfast, turn south from U.S. Highway 1 onto Maine Highway 24 at Cook's Corner east of Brunswick. After 4.4 miles, turn left onto Cundy's Harbor Road and 3.2 miles later turn right onto Bethel Point Road. The driveway to the bed & breakfast is on the left after 1.6 miles, just before the road ends at a boat ramp in the water.

To reach H2Outfitters, depart U.S. Highway 1 as if you were driving to Bethel Point, but stay on Highway 24 to the end of Orr's Island. The outfitter is on the right just before the cribstone bridge that crosses to Bailey Island.

Accommodations and reservations: Reservations are recommended at both locations. Grey Havens Inn is only open April to December. Grey Havens Inn, Seguinland Road, Georgetown Island, ME 04548, Tel. (207) 371-2616; Bethel Point Bed & Breakfast, RR 5, Bethel Point Road, Box 2387, Brunswick, ME 04011, Tel. (888) 238-8262.

Maps: Charts published by the National Oceanic and Atmospheric Administration (NOAA) are strongly recommended for coastal kayaking. For the Grey Havens area, including Sheepscot Bay, NOAA chart #13293; for Bethel Point, including Casco Bay, NOAA chart #13290.

For further information: H2Outfitters, PO Box 72, Orr's Island, ME 04066, Tel. (207) 833-5257; The Maine Island Trail Association, P.O. Box C, Rockland, ME 04841, Tel. (207) 596-6456.

10. Bascom Lodge

Mount Greylock, Massachusetts

Mount Greylock at a glance

Destination: A traditional lodge at the top of the highest summit in Massachusetts

Location: Northwestern Massachusetts, about five miles south of Williamstown and North Adams

Access: Paved road to the top of Mount Greylock

Difficulty: Easy, with Moderate options

Accommodations: Comfortable private rooms and shared coed bunkrooms

Duration: Day hikes or overnight

Featured attractions: Berkshire views, waterfalls, and varied trails in a wooded mountain preserve

A windblown summit looming in mists and tracked by the Appalachian Trail, yet visited by tourists who step out of their cars dressed in casual clothes. The top of Mount Greylock clearly presents a massive contradiction: universal access to the highest point in southern New England, combined with trails that offer the best in backcountry recreation. Thousands of acres, 7 summits, more than 35 miles of hiking trails, and a National Natural Landmark fill Mount Greylock State Reservation, a 100-year-old preserve that grandly straddles Mount Greylock's distinctive peak.

Flanked by the Hoosic River to the east and the Green River to the west, the Greylock massif runs north to south as a steep-sided mountain range, dropping abruptly into bordering valleys, yet tapering at either end, where auto roads snake to the top. The net result is a well-traveled summit that hovers above the world and calmly peers down on historic towns that huddle beneath the peak. Through-hikers on the Appalachian Trail, family groups lured by special programs, and just plain folks seeking fabulous views visit this picturesque mountain, where easy walks circle a summit tower and challenging climbs on a network of trails attract hikers of all descriptions.

Built of fieldstone and hand-hewn oak by the Civilian Conservation Corps, Bascom Lodge provides shelter in traditional mountain style just

Bascom Lodge, a traditional mountain shelter

yards beneath the spacious crest of Mount Greylock's 3491-foot summit. Owned by the Massachusetts Department of Environmental Management and operated by the Appalachian Mountain Club, a trading post, snack bar, and bustling parlor serve the general public, while private chambers, bunkrooms, shared baths, and a sunny dining hall tend to overnight guests from mid-May to mid-October. Guided hikes, nature programs, workshops, Tuesday barbecues, and Friday music nights add spice to a Bascom visit, but many guests are quite content to relax on the cozy porch and watch the glow of the setting sun beyond New York's Taconic Range.

A stone tower capped by a beacon is a little hard to miss. Rising 100 feet above the lawn just behind Bascom Lodge, the sleek profile of the War Memorial Tower serves as a logical starting point of any Greylock tour. Centered on the very peak, the circular base of this stately structure invites circumnavigation, picnics on its lawns, and wandering walks to nearby nooks and crannies with bird's-eye views of miniature towns in the valley beneath your feet. Inside the tower, metal stairs spiral walkers to an enclosed observation deck, where still more impressive vistas radiate 360 degrees to the Adirondacks of New York, the Green Mountains of Vermont, and the far corners of the rolling uplands that cover central New England.

The Appalachian Trail crosses the summit in the vicinity of the tower lawn, a taste of easy adventure that descends through evergreen scrub and crosses a web of unofficial paths that lace the mountaintop. For a touch of more vigorous hiking, try a 2.5-mile loop on the Hopper Trail and the Overlook Trail that drops sharply about 600 feet and skirts the rim of "the Hopper" before returning to the peak. A gouged cleft in the flank of the mountain that resembles a giant grain chute, the rugged Hopper shelters within its 1600 acres an old-growth stand of red spruce now recognized as a National Natural Landmark. Following the contours of Greylock's slopes between Notch and Rockwell roads, the Overlook Trail peers across the top of this mammoth void with handsome westward views of Mount Prospect and Stony Ledge on the fringe of the reservation.

For moderate walks, a trio of waterfalls offers a fine selection of outings — short, steep excursions to delicate, misty sites. Money Brook Falls is the tallest of the three. A little south of the most northerly point where the Appalachian Trail crosses the access road, find a blue-blazed path that leaves a parking turnout on the west side of Notch Road. This angled path soon intercepts Money Brook Trail, where hikers turn left, looping south and east, as they descend 300 feet. Don't be confused by a splashing brook that passes another junction. Turn left and press on to a boulder-strewn stream and an airy web of water that masks the solid-rock face of a 60-foot woodland falls.

The other two falls, Deer Hill and March Cataract, lie on opposite sides of Sperry Road, a gravel lane that traces the crest of a mountain ridge and angles away from Rockwell Road about 1.6 miles southwest of the summit. For drive-in camping, Sperry Road also provides access to Sperry Campground, a great alternative for hikers who like spacious, natural sites and immediate access to several trailheads.

On the very edge of the camping area, southwest of Sperry Road, a small bridge spans a brook near signs for Deer Hill Falls. From here, two short but energetic loops set out to explore the upper watershed of Roaring Brook. At 0.8 mile, the Circular Trail is only about half the length of the Deer Hill loop, but both discover rills and rivulets, and steeply angled woodlands that burst with wildflowers in season. Beyond a second bridge, the Deer Hill Trail tracks the tight ravine of a curling brook with a series of small cascades before crossing Roaring Brook and reclaiming 700 feet of elevation on its return to Sperry Road.

For the most beauty with the least effort, take the March Cataract Trail northeast of Sperry Road just opposite the campground contact station. Signed as a mile, but really substantially shorter, this rocky path bounces up and over a low ridge before plummeting downhill beneath giant maples, ash, and birch that cling to folds in the mountain's flank. At the end of the trail you'll find a leafy glade, cooled by the mists of a fragile falls that sprays a rock facade, enveloped by ferns, flowers, moss, and a glimpse of nearby peaks. After climbing back to the trailhead, don't leave the campground without driving or walking less than a mile down Sperry Road for a picnic at Stony Ledge. Easily accessible and dotted with wooden tables, this popular boulder outcrop offers superb northward views and a perfect perspective across the Hopper to Mount Greylock's rounded top.

Energetic hikers determined to walk Mount Greylock from bottom to top can choose from a number of trails, but the classic assault begins in simple pastures at the bottom of the Hopper. Patching together a circular route on the Money Brook, Hopper, Deer Hill, and Appalachian trails, an 11-mile circuit parallels streams spilling down from slopes that flank the

Hopper, circles the steep abyss, and traces the high ridge from Greylock's summit to Mt. William's northern peak. Bascom Lodge, Money Brook Falls, tower views, and wild, wooded slopes all appear as highlights on this hike, but the day's most memorable image is visible from at the trailhead. Easing through a farm gate beneath a giant shading maple, passing a rusting Chevy and curious dairy calves, the Money Brook and Hopper trails skim a field with the clearest view of the mountain's most distinctive feature. Seen from a grassy meadow, Greylock, Mount Prospect and Stony Ledge encircle a massive chute on a slope of dark green woods; a perfect likeness of grain being poured into Greylock's colossal Hopper.

War Memorial Tower on the summit of Mount Greylock

The practical guide

Access: Notch Road provides access to Bascom Lodge and the summit of Mount Greylock from the north. Beginning at the junction of Massachusetts Highways 2 and 8 in North Adams, drive 1.3 miles west on Highway 2 and turn left (south) onto Notch Road. Bear left at a fork after 0.55 mile and turn hard left after 1.2 miles, following signs for Mt. Greylock Reservation. Turn left again at the junction with Rockwell Road near the summit. Bascom Lodge is 9.3 miles from Highway 2.

From the south, North Main Street intersects US Highway 7 1.3 miles north of the town of Lanesborough. Follow North Main Street and then Rockwell road 2 miles to the Mt. Greylock Visitor Center for maps and interpretive information. Pass the junction with Sperry Road after 7.9 miles, and turn right at the junction with Notch Road near the summit. Bascom Lodge is 9.5 miles from US Highway 7.

The Money Brook and Hopper trailhead is located off Hopper Road and Massachusetts Highway 43. From the junction of Notch Road and Highway 2, drive 3.7 miles west on Highway 2 and turn left onto Highway 43 (Green River Road). Bear left onto Hopper Road after 2.6 miles, and bear left again 1.4 miles later where Potter Road forks right. Continue 0.8 mile on this gravel road to trailhead parking on the right.

Accommodations and reservations: Reservations are necessary at Bascom Lodge, but might be available on short notice. For advance reservations and information call (413) 443-0011. For reservations during the current week only call (413) 743-1591. Rates for bunkroom space and private rooms differ, and higher rates apply on weekends and during August. Blankets, sheets, and towels are provided. Meals are charged separately. Breakfast, dinner, and trail lunches are available daily, but specific meal reservations must also be made in advance.

Maps: A selection of maps is available at Bascom Lodge and the visitor center. Winter and summer trail maps are produced by Mt. Greylock State Reservation, and a relief map showing hiking trails is prepared by the Appalachian Mountain Club (See addresses below). The "Mt. Greylock Map" published by New England Cartographics seems easiest to use. It's available at the lodge or by writing New England Cartographics, P.O. Box 9369, N. Amherst, MA 01059.

For further information: Bascom Lodge, P.O. Box 1800, Lanesboro, MA 01237, Tel. (413) 443-0011; Mt. Greylock State Reservation, P.O. Box 138, Lanesborough, MA 01237, Tel. (413) 499-4262; The Appalachian Mountain Club, 5 Joy Street, Boston, MA 02108, Tel. (617) 523-0636.

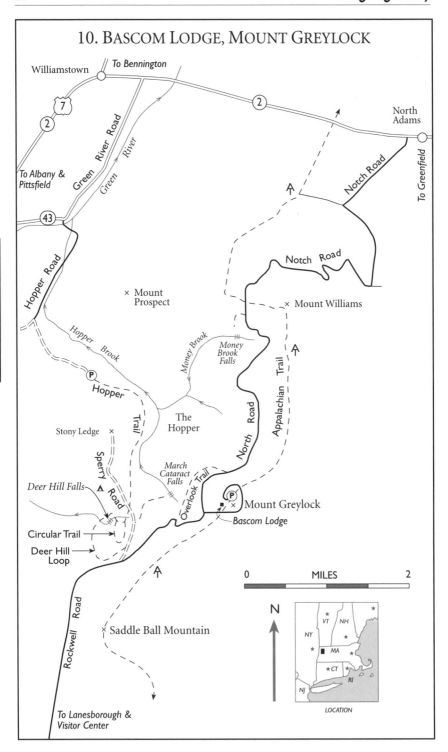

10. BASCOM LODGE, MOUNT GREYLOCK

Williamstown

To Bennington

To Albany &
Pittsfield

7
2
43

Green River Road

Green River

Green River

Hopper Road

× Mount
Prospect

Hopper   Brook

P

Hopper

Stony Ledge ×

Sperry Road

Deer Hill Falls

Circular Trail

Deer Hill
Loop

Money Brook

Money
Brook
Falls

The
Hopper

March
Cataract
Falls

Overlook Trail

North Road

Notch   Road

× Mount Williams

Appalachian Trail

Notch Road

North
Adams

To Greenfield

2

P
× Mount Greylock

Bascom Lodge

Rockwell Road

× Saddle Ball Mountain

To Lanesborough &
Visitor Center

0   MILES   2

N

VT   NH

NY

MA

★ CT

RI

NJ

LOCATION

11. Cape Cod National Seashore

Provincetown and Truro, Massachusetts

Cape Cod at a glance

Destination: Inn or bed and breakfast near a sandy seacoast preserve.
Location: Between Cape Cod Bay and the Atlantic Ocean, at the northern
  tip of Cape Cod
Access: Bike or drive to trailhead beaches
Difficulty: Easy to Moderate, depending on length of hike
Accommodations: Comfortable to casually elegant
Duration: Day hike, with overnight stays in nearby towns
Featured attractions: Ocean beaches, windswept dunes, and the natural
  history of the outer cape

From the narrow strand of Nauset Beach near Chatham at Cape Cod's
elbow to the very tip of its cupped fingers that curl inward at Provincetown
Harbor, 40 miles of beaches, dunes, and glacial uplands lie preserved in
the Cape Cod National Seashore. More than 350 years of European history preceded that preservation. Private homes and individual holdings
still exist within the preserve, distracting at times, but useful contrast to
the beauty that remains. South of Highland Light, wave-cut cliffs, narrow
beaches, and exceptional tides impede shore-front hiking. For great tramp-
ing along beaches and dunes, travel north to Cape Cod's wrist.

In 1849, Henry David Thoreau found "naked Nature" at the edge of
an ocean wilderness when he visited this moveable desert that was carried here by wind and tide from lower portions of the cape. Modern visitors might take heed of Thoreau's prophetic words when they walk this
sandy spit. In the crush of summer crowds, wildlife and naked nature
could be limited to the two-legged kind. Provincetown literally lies at the
end of the road and enjoys a reputation that corresponds to its location.
Traditional lovers of nature should arrive with an open mind, and not at
the height of the summer season. As Thoreau discovered on his famous
trip in early October, a visit in spring or fall is best for quiet hikes.

On one level, at least, there's no reason to walk the eight miles from
the Head of the Meadows to Race Point except out of sheer perversity.
Most visitors to the Cape Cod National Seashore drive into a beach-front
lot and thoroughly enjoy listless days lolling in the sun and sand. National Park Service rangers who staff the visitor centers even tend to dis-
pense odd looks when you ask about long-distance hikes. But if you're
here to uncover the wild cape that Henry Thoreau observed, the standard
reception is a promising sign that you're headed in the right direction.

Shipwreck scavengers, oystermen, and fleets of mackerel schooners
no longer frequent this hazardous coast, but a leisurely journey along the
shore still exposes timeless details of shape and texture. Pipers, plovers,

gulls, and swallows; bayberry, plum, beach grass, and dusty miller; mussels and crabs, castoffs from the ocean, and the growling sound of the sea exist in a stark landscape of subtle transformations. You'll miss the fine points if you hurry past. Take a slow walk along the shore and focus beyond the breakers from time to time where ships float on the far horizon and finback, minke, and humpback whales cruise the coast in seasonal migrations.

The best places to access this strip of sand are at Head of the Meadows Beach a little north of Highland Light on the forearm of the cape, and at Race Point Beach, near Provincetown on the back of the peninsula's hand. Lots of parking and public phones are provided at both locations. Its easy to stash a car at either end or simply walk one way, planning to call a cab or a friend to take you back to where you began. Shuttle buses operate between the beaches, North Truro, and Provincetown on a seasonal schedule. Local taxis regularly visit Provincetown Airport within sight of Race Point, and paved paths also connect Race Point to the edge of town. Logistical options are endless, especially if you ride a bike, and comfortable lodging is easy to locate in several neighboring towns. With its wealth of restaurants and accommodations, I chose to stay in Provincetown, leave a bike at Race Point, and work my way back to home base by starting at the Head of the Meadows.

Trapped between the last vestiges of pitch pine on the hills of the lower cape and the rolling dunes of beach grass that form Provincetown hook, a narrow path curls beside cedar posts as it leaves the northern end of the Head of the Meadows parking lot bound for the ocean surf. Clambering up the sandy path, hikers also spot an unpaved fire road that meanders inland through beach-front dunes, and makes a useful alternative for later in your trip. From the top of the bank, a gleaming line of ocean foam stretches out of sight, while herring gulls and lobster buoys bob beyond the breakers. Whether scrunching slowly through soft footing or making time on tide-packed sand, hikers encounter clues to the untamed power of this raw environment. Storm-tossed drift wood bakes at the base of sandy dunes, gulls feed on detritus caught in seaweed drift, and relics from other places and times attest to the hardships of life at sea. Undercut, roots exposed, their days clearly numbered, scrub oaks on a sandy bank act as vivid reminders that wind, wave, and weather make this beach a place of change.

Shallow breaks in the oceanfront dunes suggest that it's time to leave the shore. Pockmarked paths in the drifted sand lead through natural gaps to interlaced trails and fire roads that parallel the unseen coast. A warmer, dryer habitat on the back side of the beachfront banks hosts a dazzling array of plants that add to your repertoire. In the fall, beach pea, crowberry, seaside goldenrod, and the frosted parsley look of dusty miller intertwine with the scarlet leaves that make poison ivy attractive. Step carefully and consider long pants when you walk these narrow paths that meander to the edge of Salt Meadow Marsh, where swamp azalea, shad-

Pilgrim Monument and Provincetown Harbor

bush, and winterberry tangle the banks of East Harbor Creek cut off now forever from tides and the open sea.

If you get too hot in the arid dunes or the mosquitoes drive you away, return to the windswept beach, where clam shells, polished stones, and fewer footprints greet your progress. Enjoying beachcombing at its finest, you're alone with flocks of gulls, pipers darting at water's edge, and the sweep of a far horizon that bends to the curve of the earth. A sand-packed glove or a bit of debris intrudes on your reverie as slashes of white hundreds of yards offshore pinpoint shifting shoals so hazardous to navigation.

Near a bump in the coast as you round to the west on Cape Cod's wrist, an exit for off-road vehicles connects hikers to a dune-top fire road. Beach grass predominates on this breezy bench atop the sandy cliffs, but beach plums and salt-spray roses add dashes of lavish color. Swallows weave the air above the banks, dainty footprints of rabbit and fox prove the presence of wildlife, and vast panoramas open in all directions. From a height of land that rises only another 20 feet, landmarks of the outer cape spring briskly into view: Highland Light near the trailhead, the Pilgrim Monument in central Provincetown, and the hazy shore of coastal Massachusetts on the far side of Cape Cod Bay. The easy walking lane also leads to a string of shacks nestled in the dunes. Respect the privacy of the residents of these ramshackle weathered huts, holdovers from an earlier age that no doubt resemble the emergency shelters that Thoreau so eagerly found.

Perceptions of scale falter in a foreign landscape. Dead ahead, the conspicuous profile of the Old Harbor Life Saving Museum at Race Point marks the finish of your seaside journey, but distance deceives your senses. Soft footing and unrecognized miles postpone the end of your walk for almost another two hours. Bring lots of food and plenty of water on this slow, thirsty hike to fully enjoy a long day ambling at your leisure.

More than 3000 ships came to an end in the treacherous waters off this coast, and the United States Life Saving Service once manned up to 13 stations on Cape Cod's shores. Before heading back to town, wander through the Old Harbor museum for a look at the colorful history of these "Guardians of the Ocean Graveyard" who concluded their service only after the Cape Cod Canal diverted the bulk of the shipping traffic.

From the former lifesaving station, a bike path between Race Point Beach and Herring Cove Beach connects in turn to a short stretch of Highway 6 for the final link to Provincetown. Even on foot, this paved route is a worthwhile excursion, but beach walkers will already be tired enough. Bike or drive back to your lodging and save this hike for another day. In spite of all the sand you've crossed, this 2.6-mile link adds a new dimension to your understanding of the natural history of the Cape Cod dunes. As you pedal along the path, stands of pitch pine and black oak segue to laurel and cedar near shallow inland bogs and transition again into delicate plants of pastel hues that duck beneath a steady wind in steep-cut hills of sand.

Public phones, a bathhouse, and plenty of parking make Herring Cove Beach an alternate end point of your hike, but it's less than a mile from Provincetown. I ended my day by pedaling Highway 6 and spending the night as close as possible to the spot where the Pilgrims first touched this continent. Forget the fame of Plymouth Rock, the Provincetown Inn sits directly across the street from a plaque that commemorates the site where the Pilgrims landed on November 11, 1620. With stunning views of Provincetown, the harbor, and Long Point Light, the Provincetown Inn is an old-style family resort subtly removed from the hustle and bustle of the downtown commercial center, yet one of the town's most popular walks waits just outside its door.

Laid up with flat-top stones stretching nearly a mile into the harbor, a massive breakwater angles across tidal flats and connects Provincetown to a pebble beach that curls to Wood End Light. Gulls feast on fish trapped by falling tides, saltwater anglers cast for blues in the depths off the churning coast, and couples find private moments on quiet walks to the outermost lights. It's a terrific spot to begin or end a Cape Cod day. Just be aware that high tides can sometimes submerge the dike and strand hikers on the spit of gravel that bends into the harbor to form Cape Cod's fingertips.

The practical guide

Access: U.S. Highway 6 is Cape Cod's main artery. Once on the outer cape, it's the only option for travelers to Provincetown. Head of the Meadows Beach, Race Point, and Herring Cove Beach are all directly off U.S. 6 on access roads that are well marked by National Park Service signs. Summer traffic can be horrendous; all the more reason to schedule an off-season visit.

The breakwater walk to Wood End Light

Scheduled air service links Boston's Logan Airport and the Provincetown Airport at Race Point. Contact Cape Air at (800) 352-0714. Passenger ferry service is also available seasonally between Boston and Provincetown. Call Bay State Cruise Company, Inc. at (617) 723-7800.

Accommodations and reservations: Motels, hotels, inns, rooming houses, and bed and breakfasts of all shapes, sizes, and descriptions are readily available in Provincetown. Reservations are a good idea at any time of year, but mandatory during the summer. The Provincetown Chamber of Commerce publishes an annual guide to sights and services that includes accommodations. The Cape Cod Chamber of Commerce provides similar information. Both addresses are listed below.

The Provincetown Inn at One Commercial Street, Provincetown, MA 02657, is a large, waterfront, motor-inn family resort at the edge of the National Seashore and a thankful mile from the night life in the center of town. For reservations only, call 1-800-WHALE VU. Elegant accommodations at the southern end of this seashore hike are provided by South Hollow Vineyard Bed and Breakfast on Highway 6A in North Truro a little south of the junction with Highland Road. There, a marvelous breakfast patio, sumptuous surroundings, and a wine-tasting room add to a Cape Cod stay. For information and reservations call (508) 487-6200.

Backcountry adventurers should note that camping and open fires are not permitted in the Cape Cod National Seashore.

Maps: An Official Map and Guide to Cape Cod National Seashore is available at the Salt Pond Visitor Center and the Province Lands Visitor Center, both off U.S. Highway 6. For advance information contact Cape Cod National Seashore at the address below.

For further information: Superintendent, Cape Cod National Seashore, South Wellfleet, MA 02663, Tel. (508) 349-3785; Cape Cod Chamber of Commerce, Hyannis, MA 02601, Tel. (508) 362-3225; Provincetown Chamber of Commerce, P.O. Box 1017, Provincetown, MA 02657, Tel. (508) 487-3424.

11. CAPE COD NATIONAL SEASHORE

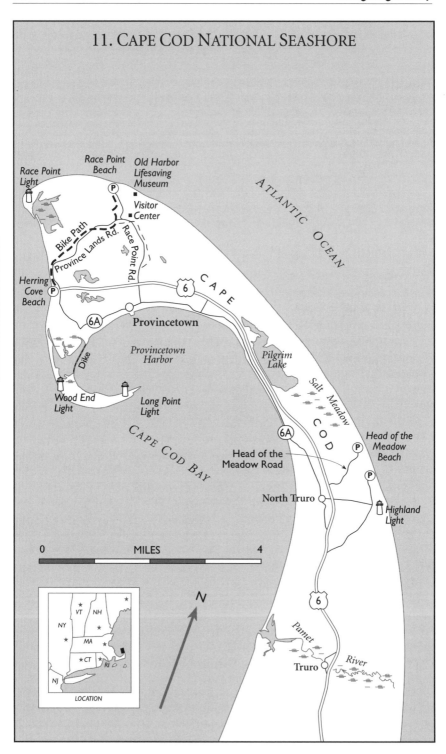

12. Mohawk Trail and Savoy Mountain State Forests

Charlemont and Florida, Massachusetts

Mohawk and Savoy state forests at a glance

Destination: Log cabins near pond or stream in the mountains of Massachusetts

Location: Five and ten miles east of North Adams in northwestern Massachusetts

Access: Variable; year-round drive to the cabin door or a half-mile winter walk, depending on choice of site

Difficulty: Easy

Accommodations: Rustic cabins

Duration: Two nights or extended stay

Featured attractions: Swimming, skiing, mountain trails, and surprising wildlife

Log cabins and backcountry trails near a highway in Massachusetts? I had my doubts too, but the howl of coyotes in the dead of night brought a rapid reassessment. Make no mistake — the Hoosac Range along with the end of the Green Mountain chain that spills out of Vermont make the northwest corner of Massachusetts authentically rough terrain. Unlike the massive summits of northern New England that rise like ocean swells, the hills of Mohawk Trail and Savoy Mountain state forests adjoin in a choppy region of tightly clustered peaks that have long resisted the advance of progress in their own disordered way. More than 100 years ago, builders of railroads found it wiser to bore nearly five miles through the base of a Berkshire mountain than challenge the face of this raucous land. For backcountry enthusiasts looking for comfort, these stubby hills and steep-walled valleys are wild enough to try.

Walden Pond set the standard for contemplative waterfront housing. The cabins at Mohawk Trail and Savoy Mountain aren't really quite as secluded, but if you're looking for a chance to swim, ski, explore forest trails, and relax in a pond-side cabin, they're a very good imitation. Both of these neighboring state forests in the historic northern Berkshires offer campgrounds, cabins, woodland trails, and thousands of acres of recreation, but unique combinations of characteristics make them appealing in different ways. To maximize comfort and avoid crowds, save Savoy for summer and fall, and come to Mohawk in the dead of winter.

Mohawk Trail State Forest

Deep in a cleft below Todd Mountain, the Mohawk Trail (Massachusetts Highway 2) traces the course of the Cold River as it curls through the depths of a chiselled notch and rushes to join the Deerfield River in a race through the Pioneer Valley. Site of the first state campground in Massachusetts, the crisp stream and the rough-hewn pass still attract summer crowds for tenting and swimming under the pines in Mohawk Trail State Forest. You'll find great recreation in the heat of August, but too many people too close to the road to appeal to the backcountry crowd.

For solitude in the northern woods, come to this compact notch in deserted January, when ice chokes the stream, snow buries the camp, and even cross-country skiers forsake these vertical slopes for more suitable Nordic terrain. Follow a snow-plowed driveway up the ridge, twisting away from the frosted swimming holes, and climb to a cluster of cozy cabins that make a perfect midwinter home. Secluded in the hillside woods at the end of the road, five log cabins are specially furnished to cater to off-season guests. Enjoy the luxury of electric lights, padded bunks, toasty woodstove heat, access right to your door, and a handicap-accessible outhouse just down the road with tile floors, flush toilets, and hot showers even in the middle of winter. The experience is tame in the warmer months, but when temperatures drop, winds whistle, and coyotes bay at night, you'll welcome the creature comforts. Its a great base for cold-weather jaunts into the lonely woods or

Winter cabin, Mohawk Trail State Forest

solitary treks over untracked trails to vistas from a snow-capped ridge.

Gulf moisture overrode arctic air the night before my visit, and five inches of new snow covered the Totem Trail, one of two paths in Mohawk Trail State Forest that are perfect for winter hiking. Jumping quickly out of the valley from a stone monument on the south side of Highway 2, the Totem Trail soon strikes a moderate pace, easing through clusters of mountain laurel and evergreens as it enters a mature, well-spaced hardwood forest. Small tracks of cloven hooves blaze the way up slope, charting the comings and goings of white-tailed deer that gathered, drifted apart, and pawed for food on a mossy bank at the base of a stately oak. Bare branches in the winter stillness allow views of neighboring hills as the trail angles upward past gentle knolls and rises to a lookout with a woodsy view down the glen of Trout Brook to the distant Mohawk Trail.

A more energetic hike climbs the ridge behind the cabins. From the access road near the west end of the campground, the Indian Trail scales a slanted slope to a sag between the summits of Clark and Todd mountains. Blue-blazed, but hard to follow in crusted snow, the path climbs briskly and bends hard right before arriving at a **T** where hikers have a choice of peaks. I turned east toward Todd Mountain, traversing a fabulous ridge where thickets of mountain laurel spread beneath canopied oak — sturdy trunks and lacy shrubs underlain with winter white. The windswept crest offers dramatic vistas of frozen landscapes and rumpled peaks, but don't end your hike at the first conspicuous knoll. Push on and follow partridge tracks along a narrowing path that scrambles over the summit and dead ends at an overlook with majestic eastward views of the broad Deerfield River beginning its rapid journey through the Pioneer Valley.

Savoy Mountain State Forest

West of the entrance to Mohawk Trail State Forest, Highway 2 doubles its elevation as it climbs to the top of the Hoosac plateau and arrives in less rugged terrain. Perched at the highest levels of an eroded mountain range, 11,000-acre Savoy Mountain State Forest spans a diverse landscape, speckled with low-rising, wooded summits and laced with ponds and streams. Three rustic cabins line the shore of South Pond just west of the access road, a great destination for swimming, canoeing, angling for trout, or kicking back with a steak on the grill and savoring a summer day.

Over 20 miles of hiking trails weave through this scattered forest, welcome diversions in cool woodlands in the heat of an August day. For a moderate hike and excellent views from the highest (natural) point in Savoy Mountain State Forest, walk the Busby Trail, which climbs Spruce Hill after leaving Old Florida Road, a dirt lane that intersects Central Shaft Road at a sharp turn just beyond the Forest Headquarters. White-birch glades, Staples Brook, and the stone-lined pit of a cellar hole mark this gentle ascent. Nearing the top, choose the north fork of a trail that splits to form a loop. This newer fork takes a more gradual route that avoids outcrop boulders as it circles to slanting facets of slab and vistas from a slender peak. Allow plenty of time for a leisurely orientation at the top. Check the Green Mountain summits that rise in the north, the unmistakable mound of Mount Greylock that dominates the west, and the full panorama of Berkshire County that falls away to the south. Keep a sharp eye too on the arching sky where hawks and eagles pass overhead as they migrate every fall.

Other trails explore the everyday wilderness of

North Pond, Savoy Mountain State Forest

these hidden Berkshire woods. Just outside your cabin door, two loops circle North Pond and Tyler Swamp, where bears, birds, and wildflowers appear along four-season paths that penetrate the mundane regions where wildlife congregates. Blessed with varied habitats, Savoy Mountain State Forest is packed with a fine selection of mixed-use trails blazed for both hiking and skiing, but visitors may find the South Pond cabins too rustic for winter use. From mid-May to mid-October, the cabins share water, showers, and sanitary facilities with a nearby campground, but you're on your own in winter, with only a composting toilet, no water, no electricity, and about a 0.5-mile walk to the road. For cross-country skiing and a comfortable winter option, rent a cabin at Mohawk Trail and commute to the year-round tracks that web Savoy.

The practical guide

Access: The entrance to Mohawk Trail State Forest is 4.2 miles west of the village of Charlemont on the north side of Massachusetts Highway 2 (The Mohawk Trail). Cabins are located beyond the contact station at the end of a well-marked spur off the campground access road.

The road to Savoy Mountain State Forest intersects Highway 2 9.5 miles west of the entrance to Mohawk Trail State Forest, and about 5 miles east of the Wigwam gift shop. About 1.0 mile west of the fire station in the town of Florida, turn south onto an unmarked road at a brown and white SAVOY STATE FOREST sign. Bear right at two successive forks following more state forest signs, and stay on Central Shaft Road as it crosses the unseen Hoosac Tunnel and arrives at forest headquarters 2.9 miles from the highway. The entrance to the campground and cabins is 1.0 mile beyond the forest headquarters. Winter visitors park near the closed campground gate and walk about 0.5 mile to the cabins.

Accommodations and reservations: Cabin reservations can be made up to six months in advance and should be made as soon as possible. Both locations require a two-night minimum stay, with a seven-night minimum (two-week maximum) during the summer season. A two-night deposit is required. Savoy offers only small one-room cabins. Mohawk offers both small cabins and larger units with separate living and sleeping areas. At this writing nightly rental fees are only $8 for small cabins, $10 for large. You'll need a sleeping bag and all of your cold-weather camping gear for winter stays, along with water, fire wood, and kindling for the stove. Complete rules, information, and reservations are available from the addresses below.

Maps: Very good trail maps are available at the respective forest headquarters and from the addresses below.

For further information: Mohawk Trail State Forest, P.O. Box 7, Charlemont, MA 01339, Tel. (413) 339-5505; Savoy Mountain State Forest, 260 Central Shaft Road, Florida, MA 01247, Tel. (413) 663-8469.

New Hampshire

13. Cardigan Lodge
Alexandria, New Hampshire

Cardigan at a glance

Destination: Campground and lodge at the base of Mt. Cardigan
Location: Near Bristol and Plymouth, New Hampshire, about 8 miles west of Newfound Lake
Access: Year-round gravel road
Difficulty: Easy to Moderate
Accommodations: Comfortable, family bunk rooms with shared showers and bath
Duration: Weekend or overnight
Featured attractions: Woodland walks and commanding views from a central New Hampshire peak

Miles removed from crowded lakes and far south of the busy White Mountains, thousands of acres of Cardigan State Park and the adjacent Cardigan Reservation occupy a forgotten corner of west-central New Hampshire. Within this obscure region, a deserted town hall surrounded by forest and gray rows of stone walls lost on wooded slopes bear testament to the passage of time. Farmers departed for greener, less rocky pastures, and interstate highways now quickly transport tourists beyond these humble summits to the highest New England peaks. Left behind is a workaday wilderness that our ancestors may have enjoyed, where deer, moose, bear, and partridge roam free in the dense woodlands of rugged New Hampshire hills.

Two-state views, moderate trails, and a bare-rock open summit have long attracted families to Mt. Cardigan. The gentler western slopes especially cater to very young hikers, who frequently make "The Sweater" their first serious summit attempt. Sequestered at the end of a long road in the private Cardigan Reservation, the Appalachian Mountain Club's (AMC's) newly spruced-up Cardigan Lodge does its part to also make the more challenging eastern slopes a setting for family hikes.

Campers will find a great selection of spacious sites in the woods beyond the lodge. Convenient drive-in locations offer families hassle-free tenting tucked into a corner of a hillside meadow or secluded in a forest

69

Cardigan Lodge, at the base of Mount Cardigan

glade. For true comfort, though, the amenities of Cardigan Lodge prove far too hard to pass up. At this three-story inn with a fireplaced great room for dining and conversation, the level of comfort exceeds that of the AMC's more familiar high peak huts. Family-sized rooms with bunks and bureaus, modern tile showers, shared baths, and a play room with views of Cardigan's peak provide elbow room and a ration of privacy. Sheets, mattresses, and family-style meals round out the hospitality at a reasonably affordable price. With a swimming hole at the trailhead and a beach at Wellington State Park just a short drive away, comfort combines with lots of attractions to entice an active family.

Of course, hiking is the main attraction. Nearly fifty miles of maintained trails lace the park and reservation. Tumbling cascades, pothole ledges, and the plunging waters of Welton Falls lure visitors east from Cardigan Lodge for half-day excursions on the lower branch of the Manning Trail. Cilley's Cave and the glacier-formed Hanging Ledges draw more ambitious hikers far north for extended treks on the slopes of Firescrew Mountain. But the crackled veins of a bald-granite mound that rises to the west convince most visitors that Mt. Cardigan and its firetower are the primary destinations.

A broad selection of well-marked paths connects the lodge to the top of this barren peak. Difficulty levels range from the arduous upper Holt Trail (to be avoided by most, even in good weather), to the longer but less demanding Skyland and Vistamont route. For a less-traveled circuit that blends the best of New Hampshire's woodlands with the thrill of a wind-swept peak, cobble together an outbound trip on the Manning and Mowglis trails with a rapid descent on the Clark, Cut-off, Vistamont, and lower Holt trails that return you to your base.

Leaving the hiker's room in the basement of Cardigan Lodge, grab a trail map off the patio, walk past the spring-fed swimming hole that sits at the meadow's edge, and follow signs for the Manning Trail along remnants of an old dirt road. Beyond scattered campsites, a yellow blaze soon turns the trail away from the ancient lane, angling northwest through stately stands of maple, beech, and birch on Firescrew Mountain's lower slopes. The springtime sun easily penetrates to the floor of this tilting forest, where wildflower carpets of yellow and white dazzle early-season guests. In time, the route curls more directly west before the upper end of the Manning Trail tackles a series of increasingly steeper pitches that carry hikers over slanting plates of barren ledge with impressive alpine views.

Named after a blaze that once engulfed the mountaintop, Firescrew Mountain stands well below Cardigan's looming peak, but the top-of-the-world feeling on this wide, flat summit imitates the aura of the Presidential Peaks at a readily accessible height. Surrounded by precarious blueberry bushes and low, stunted birch, the white-blazed path traverses a pitted surface of aging rock as it roams the summit's ledges toward the conspicuous Cardigan tower. Passing pools of water captured by glacier-scarred rock, hikers scan the majestic panorama of central New Hampshire, from the faint shadows of the White Mountains lining the northern horizon to the sparkling glint of Newfound Lake reflecting the morning sun.

The Manning Trail ends at the Mowglis junction about 0.6 mile north of Cardigan's peak. Hikers with extra time and a yen for private views can detour to the right on the Mowglis Trail and enter an emerald world of moss, spruce and labrador tea on less-visited mountain heights. Before long, this northbound branch descends steeply to crude Crag Camp, an overnight shelter that only the heartiest backpackers find appealing. Dayhikers should turn south at the Mowglis junction, quickly visit a wooded col, and then follow the moss-filled fissures and cracks in the granite of the summit cone to the top of Cardigan's windblown peak.

Isolated in a sea of wooded summits that fall away in all directions and encircled by views of Vermont's Green Mountains and New Hampshire's highest peaks, Cardigan delivers big-mountain excitement at the modest elevation of only 3121 feet. Come prepared for the chill winds and changeable weather you might expect on taller peaks, and soak in alpine pleasures attained at a moderate cost. Cracks and ridges provide ample cover for lunch in a protected lee, while the firetower serves as a natural magnet for kids of all ages. Drop your pack at its metal feet and climb its wooden stairs to the enclosed cabin that caps this working tower. A ranger might tell you all about the colors of smoke, approaching weather fronts, or the details of the vast terrain.

Just west of the tower, a signpost and painted blazes guide the Clark Trail off the cone. Bearing southeast, hikers pick their steps carefully down steep faces of rock and find more directional signs near the front of a ranger cabin. For added perspectives on the balding summit and close-up views of rugged hills that parallel the Connecticut Valley, a second detour toward South Peak and Rimrock is well worth the added effort. For the direct route

The firetower on Mount Cardigan's granite peak

back to Cardigan Lodge, continue on the Clark Trail through a tangled web of paths that connect nearby summits with the AMC High Cabin, a basic shelter just below treeline designed for year-round use. The cabin offers a kitchen, woodstove, rough bunks, table, benches, and a weather-tight roof for self-sufficient groups who are ready to pack in sleeping bags, carry all of their supplies, and make reservations in advance.

Descending rapidly down the eastern slopes, trust a sign that points to the AMC SKI LODGE and then bear left at a fork onto the Cathedral Forest Trail, also known as the Holt-Clark Cutoff. Within 0.5 mile you'll arrive at another clump of crisscross junctions. Turn left on Vistamont, ignore a ski trail, and turn right on the Holt Trail after only 0.1 mile. The final leg to Cardigan Lodge might be muddy at times, but pretty cascades in a sharp ravine make up for the inconvenience. Tracking a brook, the route crosses the water on a hiker's bridge above a peaceful glade, where gentle banks shaded by hardwoods create a pensive spot within easy reach of the trailhead; a perfect place for guests to revisit and linger on an evening stroll.

Whether camping, dayhiking, or rooming at the lodge, Cardigan makes a splendid choice for early-season expeditions and a grand option on summer days when clouds cover the White Mountain peaks. In the snowbound months, the lodge is open only on a self-service basis. Groups of cross-country skiers, snowshoers, and lovers of cold weather have a chance to wander through thousands of acres of pristine woods if they're ready to cook their own food and generally fend for themselves.

New Hampshire

The practical guide

Access: From exit 23 of Interstate 93, follow New Hampshire Highway 104 west 5 miles to the junction with New Hampshire Highway 3A in the center of Bristol. Turn right (north) on 3A and continue 2 miles to a blinker light and a church at the intersection of West Shore Road. Turn left onto West Shore Road, passing beaches and condominiums on Newfound Lake, and continue straight after 1.8 miles, following signs for Alexandria where West Shore Road turns sharply right. Mt. Cardigan soon comes into view ahead. Do *not* follow the road to Alexandria. Instead, bear right onto Fowler River Road, following AMC LODGE signs. Within the next 5.7 miles, Fowler River Road bears left at 3.2 miles, turns right onto a gravel stretch at 4.3 miles, turns right again at 4.4 miles, and eventually narrows to a one-lane road as it finally climbs to the lodge. All turns should be well marked with AMC directory signs.

Accommodations and reservations: Naturalist programs and theme weekends often fill the lodge. Be sure to write or call ahead for reservations. Cardigan Lodge & Reservation, RFD #1, Box 712, Bristol, NH 03222, Summer Tel. (603) 744-8011; Winter Tel. (603) 744-8069

Maps: USGS Mount Cardigan quad; trail maps are also available at the lodge.

For further information: Cardigan Lodge & Reservation, RFD #1, Box 712, Bristol, NH 03222, summer Tel. (603) 744-8011; Regional Manager, Cardigan State Park, Box 273, West Ossipee, NH 03890, Tel. (603) 323-2087.

New Hampshire

13. MOUNT CARDIGAN

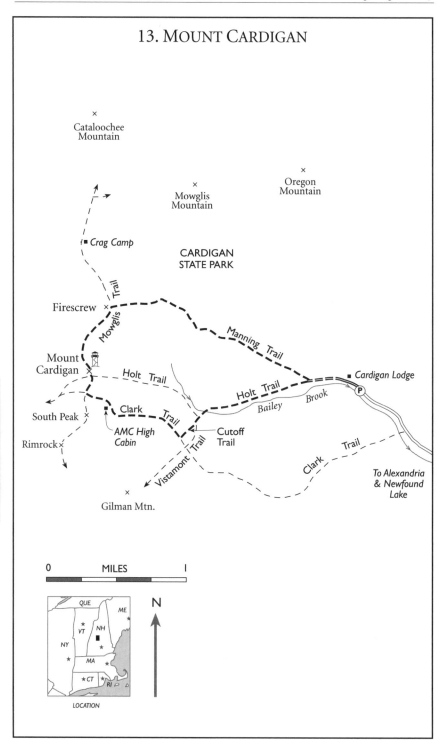

× Cataloochee Mountain

× Oregon Mountain

× Mowglis Mountain

■ Crag Camp

CARDIGAN STATE PARK

Firescrew ×

Mowglis Trail

Manning Trail

Mount Cardigan ×

Holt Trail

Holt Trail

Cardigan Lodge

South Peak ×

Clark Trail

Bailey Brook

P

AMC High Cabin

Cutoff Trail

Rimrock ×

Vistamont Trail

Clark Trail

To Alexandria & Newfound Lake

× Gilman Mtn.

0   MILES   1

QUE
ME
VT ★ NH
NY ★
MA ★
★ CT ★ RI

N

LOCATION

New Hampshire

14. The Connecticut River

Orford, New Hampshire, and Newbury and North Thetford, Vermont

The Connecticut River at a glance

Destination: Bed and breakfast inns along the Connecticut River.

Location: Connecticut River Valley between Woodsville, New Hampshire, and White River Junction, Vermont

Access: State and interstate highways to launch sites on either side of the river.

Difficulty: Easy to moderate flat-water paddling depending on distance travelled

Accommodations: Very comfortable inns, or waterfront campsites

Duration: From one to three days

Featured attractions: Fish, wildlife, waterfowl, and paddling on a rural stream.

The Connecticut Valley is rich in history and extremely old. Older than the first steam-powered vessel tested near the Orford bridge, older than a state-line survey stone installed by order of the Supreme Court, older than native birch-bark canoes paddled in King Philip's War, and older even than the grinding glaciers that terraced its hillside slopes. Well known as the sinewy border between New Hampshire and Vermont, this primeval river valley boasts truly ancient origins that are rarely understood. Separating the core of the North American continent from "exotic" island terrain that drifted across the ocean, this arcing boundary dates from the collision of tectonic plates more than 350 million years ago.

The face of the river reveals its storied past. From its source in a small woodland bog in far northern New Hampshire to its mouth on the waters of Long Island Sound on Connecticut's southern shore, the effect of human endeavor is seldom far away. The 40-mile segment centered in Orford is certainly no exception. Wilderness disappeared from this region at least two centuries ago, but after using the river for easy access, settlers turned their backs on the water and pretended it wasn't there. Meandering through channels in forgotten marshes, skirting remote pastures, and edging distant fields, the Connecticut River sneaks behind rural towns that seem oblivious to its flow. Miles of peaceful canoeing roll by in an undisturbed channel that is still nature's domain. Diverted by views of rounded mountains that parallel the quiet stream, paddlers drift past ducks, herons, otters and geese unfazed by herds of holsteins that graze along the shore.

Flat-water paddling prevails on this rural trip. Tamed by a dam at Wilder, Vermont, the Connecticut River backs up for miles as a thin, channeled lake. No exciting rapids, but there's plenty of water beneath your keel even in the driest months. You'll find perfect conditions for teaching young paddlers and newcomers to the sport, while experienced boaters might even learn how to deal with the river's quirks. During much of the season, any current that exists above Wilder Dam is impossible to detect — no help to weary paddlers, but important to keep in mind when charting your river trip. Confounding winds on summer afternoons are another consideration. Often blowing up-river from south to north, these breezes actually make downstream progress more difficult than paddling up, the equivalent to straining into the fetch of a very long, gusty lake. It makes perfect sense to paddle "upstream" in this slack-water region, and round trips from inns or waterfront campsites are also plausible schemes. Count on 3 miles per hour as an average speed for roaming this whimsical river, and be ready to adjust your plans.

Touches of civilization actually benefit river travelers. Boat launches and rest stops are frequently found near modern bridges or by the abutments of long-lost spans, and steeples in valley towns often herald country inns. In the 23 river miles between Newbury and North Thetford, five launch sites and an equal number of campgrounds line the river banks, while three traditional bed-and-breakfast inns provide overnight comfort within walking distance of shore. The size of your group, ability to spot cars, meal preference, length of stay, and general exuberance for paddling should govern your choice of plans. Mix and match launch sites and overnight stops while canoeing inn to inn, or select a base and day-trip wherever on the river you please. I began at the northern end in the village of Newbury, Vermont, and promptly headed "downstream" gaining lessons in currents and breezes with every paddle stroke.

High ceilings, polished floors, striped wallpaper, and lace-filled sunny windows typify A Century Past in Newbury village. This cozy bed and breakfast is just a pleasant stroll from the boat launch south of town, a mile-long trek that the innkeeper says "only wimps" would have trouble walking. Don't miss the garden behind the brick facade, where tables and chairs on a marvelous lawn overlook the Connecticut Valley and the summits of the White Mountains that rise in tiers beyond. It's a great spot at either end of a paddling adventure, but I proved myself a wimp, driving south through the village, turning east, and parking at a boat launch by the bridge at the edge of town.

The highest peaks disappear when you're on the water. As you float through the bends of a broad stream, beginning the journey south, stratified layers step up from parallel shores — mud, sand, a layer of hardwoods climbing a 20-foot bank, then a line of tasseled corn capped by a wispy sky. As you round another bend, feathery plumes of milkweed tumble across the surface and the low horizon expands to include the gleam of a lonely silo and the top of a nearby ridge. Twists and turns abound in this early section, until groves of oak and maple overtake a field north of Bedell Bridge.

Midstream remains of Bedell Bridge

A state park on the New Hampshire side commemorates this twice-lost span, where only a stone abutment now signals an alternate launch site that shortens your river journey by approximately three miles.

Downstream of the park, another mile brings paddlers to Vaughan Meadow, where silt and gravel terraces attest to a glacial history. Above the sweep of a sandy beach, this excellent picnic spot is the first of several campsites developed by the Upper Valley Land Trust for responsible public use. Below this rest stop and swimming hole, the geography of the valley changes once again as a granite face looms above the western shore and marks a fork in the river that paddlers might find confusing. Stay west (right as you head downstream) to stick with the main channel or continue straight if you want a long dead-end digression thick with flowering lily pads and the promise of wildlife.

A cluster of steeples at the base of a hill heralds the town of Bradford, where an arcing frame of a railroad bridge spans the mouth of the Waits River. A boat launch and campsite encroach on a field about a mile up this tributary, but it's a busy spot at the edge of town and not really recommended. Better to push on for another mile beyond the Bradford-Piermont Bridge (Highway 25C), as white pine and birch add color to the wooded banks, and the private channel slides past Piermont village, contorting in rapid bends to a camp known as Underhill. Caught on a low bank between the river and Eastman Creek, this superb site overlooks a hidden marsh that exploded with ducks as soon as my boat touched its muddy shore. Marked by a yellow sign and complete with a picnic table, Underhill Campsite catches warm breezes that keep pesky bugs at bay as you take in the reedy wetlands and the sweep of the river course.

South of Piermont, the river noticeably widens and the great granite faces of Orford soar steeply above the flow. In the last few miles before town, the first buildings to front on the water since back at Bedell Bridge intrude on waterfowl. The steel arch of a tilted span angles across the river between Orford, New Hampshire, and Fairlee, Vermont, connecting towns that look like they were meant to ignore each other. Paddle 0.25 mile past the slanted bridge just beyond a series of docks reserved for a private campground. To the left, on the eastern shore, a public dock and boat launch opens onto a grassy lawn where cars and canoes are easily stowed for the night. Head up the gravel lane to New Hampshire Highway 10 for a leg-stretching walk of only 0.6 mile that leads to the White Goose Inn.

New Hampshire

A red-brick bed and breakfast, the White Goose Inn offers post-and-beam comfort in traditional colonial style. Known for a tree that once grew through the roof of its front porch, this historic home invites guests to share a restful ambience that matches a relaxed decor. After a hard day on the river, canoeists sleep soundly in rooms with private baths but no telephone or TV. Breakfast is served each morning, but guests without cars should make special arrangements for transport to an evening meal.

In the final third of the journey, cattails, reeds, and lily pads appear along the shore as canoes drift by Birch Meadow campsite two miles south of Orford. Settled above a marsh near the outlet of Lake Morey, this waterfront camp peers out over dead calm water where ducks mingle with mirrored reflections until bursting into flight. The return to civilization is gradual as you cruise between wooded banks that hold an increasing number of homes sprouting on opposite shores. The sweet smell of sawdust foretells a lumber mill around a sweeping turn before a long straight paddle arrives at the outlet of Clay Brook, a short backwater stream with a novel view of a covered bridge across a shallow pool. Back on the southbound river, the sound of cars on US Highway 5 soon lets you know that it's time to end your journey. Paddle around the back of North Thetford to the stone piling of a missing bridge stranded in mid-river. Follow the easy curve of Vermont's shore until the takeout comes into view, a wooden dock and boat launch at the base of a grassy bank.

Merely yards from the dock, the Stone House Inn in North Thetford is without doubt the most convenient lodge on the trip, with porches and cozy verandas sporting pond and river views. The owners are experienced river hands, and canoeists are warmly welcomed to rooms with shared baths, high tin ceilings, and lots of Victorian charm. Breakfast is served,

A Connecticut Valley view

New Hampshire

but not an evening meal. Count on driving a car to delightful dining in the college town of Hanover, and you've created the perfect spot for lingering summer weekends or a very relaxed conclusion to an easy river cruise.

Miles of flat water lie south of North Thetford all the way to the Wilder Dam. Three more campsites and six public boat launches fill this popular section. Be forewarned, though, the miles through bustling Hanover are too civilized for many paddlers. If you choose to pass this way, be sure to stop at the Ledyard Canoe Club. It's the oldest collegiate canoe club in America — a very good source for lessons and a place to rent a canoe.

The practical guide

Access: Interstate Highway 91 parallels the western edge of the Connecticut Valley in Vermont. Use Exit 14 for North Thetford, Exit 15 for Orford, and Exit 16 for Bradford and Newbury. US Highway 5 shadows the river in Vermont, while New Hampshire Highway 10 runs along the New Hampshire side. Highway bridges cross the river at Woodsville, Newbury, Bradford-Piermont, Orford-Fairlee, East Thetford-Lyme, and Hanover.

The Ledyard Canoe Club is located off Interstate 91, Exit 13 in New Hampshire at the end of the bridge in New Hampshire.

Accommodations and reservations: Reservations are a must at any small inn or bed and breakfast in this heavily traveled region. A Century Past requires additional arrangements if dinner is expected. Located on Main Street (US Highway 5) just north of the town common. No smoking, no pets, no children under 12. Open May through November. Route 5, Newbury, VT 05051, Tel. (802) 866-3358; White Goose Inn Located just south of the village on Highway 10. No smoking, no pets, discourages children under eight. Open year-round. Route 10, P.O. Box 17, Orford, NH 03777, Tel. (800) 358-4267; Stone House Inn Located just off US Highway 5 at a sharp turn on the south edge of town. Smoking on first floor only. No pets. Open year-round. Route 5, North Thetford, VT 05054, Tel. (802) 333-9124

Maps: USGS Newbury, Piermont, Fairlee, and Lyme quads

For further information: For campers, Upper Valley Land Trust, 19 Buck Road, Hanover, NH 03755, Tel. (603) 643-6626; For rentals and instruction, The Ledyard Canoe Club, PO Box 9, Robinson Hall, Hanover, NH 03755, Tel. (603) 643-6709.

New Hampshire

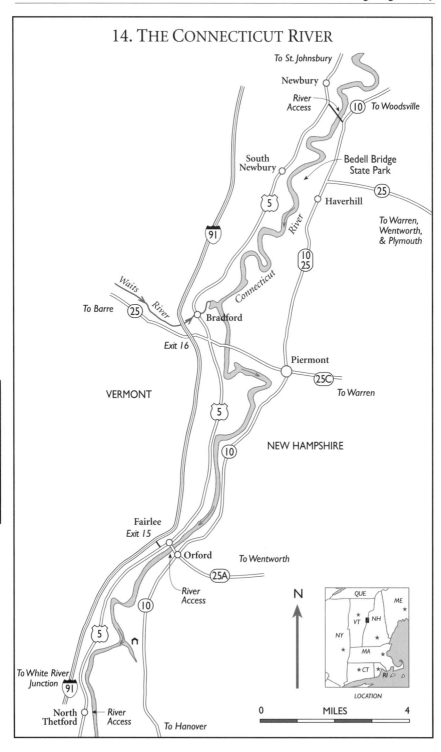

14. THE CONNECTICUT RIVER

15. Gray Knob and Crag Camp
White Mountains, New Hampshire

Crag Camp at a glance

Destination: Huts and cabins in the Presidential Range in White Mountain National Forest

Location: Northern New Hampshire, about 8 miles west of Gorham

Access: Highway to the trailhead, mountain paths to the camps

Difficulty: Moderate

Accommodations: A range of options from a rough Adirondack shelter to a snug winterized cabin

Duration: Two or three days

Featured attractions: Alpine lawns, glorious views, Mount Jefferson and Mount Adams

Located at the northern base of the Presidential Peaks on the edge of a national forest, the town of Randolph has long attracted vigorous alpine hikers. Continuing a proud tradition, the Randolph Mountain Club maintains a network of trails and a series of backcountry camps scattered along a prominent ridge that rises to Mount Adams. Less well known than the alpine huts of the Appalachian Mountain Club (AMC), the Randolph camps are better suited to self-sufficient hikers who can do without prepared meals and pressurized running water. For those who can take their mountains straight, options range from a crude hut that clings to an upper slope to the most glorious camp in the White Mountains on the lip of King Ravine.

A huge glacial cirque carved into a northern slope, King Ravine serves as a rough and tumble divide of sheer walls and massive boulders. To the east, the Valley Way and other trails ascend Durand Ridge on the way to Madison Spring (See Chapter 17), while to the west, historic routes climb moderate Nowell Ridge, which leads along a broad flank to the summit of Mount Adams. The 5.2 mile route described here pieces together sections of three trails west of King Ravine that pass four overnight huts offering various levels of comfort, and climb to Edmands Col, a high, narrow link on the spine of the Presidential Range just below New Hampshire's second and third highest peaks. For an extended exploration of some of New England's finest alpine sights, well-prepared hikers have the option of combining this trip with a night at Madison Spring by crossing the summit of Mount Adams and descending one of the several trails east of King Ravine.

The most direct route to the Randolph camps begins on Lowe's Path, a storied trail built by Charles Lowe and Dr. William Nowell more than 120 years ago. From the side of U.S. Highway 2 (See **Access** below), follow a jeep track into the woods for about 50 yards. A large sign marks the junction where Lowe's Path branches right, crossing an abandoned railroad bed and passing a powerline while hikers warm up gradually and the sound of the highway fades. After 1.6 miles, Lowe's Path crosses a brook and turns sharply left. Climbing steeply up stone stairs, the trail converges with The Link, an alternate path that connects Lowe's Path to the Appalachia trailhead and various routes east of King Ravine.

Pass a trail that branches left to the floor of King Ravine. Then continue straight for another mile on the mostly moderate path that scrambles steeply for a short stint to glimpses of northern summits and crosses still another trail within sight of the Log Cabin. A spacious hut that would be enclosed if it had a large front door, the comfort level of this Randolph camp shades to the rougher side. Rebuilt in 1985 in a hillside glade, the Log Cabin offers double-decker floor space, a fire ring, and protection from wind and rain. It's better than a tent, and great for hardy hikers, but much more pleasurable options are less than a mile away.

Beyond the Log Cabin, an 0.7-mile section of trail climbs steeply at times and flirts with being difficult. Forge straight ahead near the start of this stretch and cross the Randolph Path, a more direct route to Edmands Col that misses the next two camps. A tough climb is soon forgotten as Lowe's Path breaks from the woods and levels off on the approach to Gray Knob. With superb views of the Jefferson Highlands and the serrated profile of Castellated Ridge descending from Mount Jefferson, Lowe's Path rises to the top of a bulge where a left turn onto the Quay Path leads in short order to the cozy Gray Knob cabin.

Tucked snugly into a forest opening at a junction of mountainous trails, Gray Knob is a modern two-story cabin that serves White Mountains hikers at any time of year. Heated by a wood stove only in winter, this homey shelter features tables and benches on the first floor with a sink and counters for cooking, and a second-story loft with a dozen or so mattresses that are spread around the floor. Just below timberline at 4400 feet, Gray Knob is perfectly suited to the needs of winter hikers, who are sternly warned to leave crampons outside the cabin door.

For summer hikers, the crown jewel of the Randolph camps lies 0.4 mile east. From the front of Gray Knob cabin, follow the Gray Knob Trail on an easy detour that descends to pass a spring and withdraws from crowding conifers at the back of Crag Camp. Newly constructed in 1993, this remarkable cabin is the latest incarnation of structures that have stood on this prominent site since 1909. Tile kitchen countertops, bunkrooms for four to eight, and high ceilings in a great room with picture-window views make this spacious cabin unique. Walk onto the front deck or a nearby overlook knoll, and the view is overwhelming. King Ravine falls at your feet, dropping 1600 feet, while high above the headwall on the opposite side of the cirque, Mount Madison and Mount Adams more than double the depth of the chasm.

When it's time to leave Crag Camp, backtrack to Gray Knob cabin. Follow the Quay Path until the Gray Knob Trail bears left, a shortcut that

Crag Camp, near the lip of King Ravine

returns to Lowe's Path a little above the Quay Path junction. From this intersection, Lowe's Path leads directly to Mount Adams. To complete the final 1.8 miles to the hub of Edmands Col, walk the rocky, rough, but relatively level Gray Knob Trail, which edges around a shoulder of Mount Adams and skirts another ravine. Well above timberline, there's lots of exposure as you work around this contour and spot a glint of sun on the Perch (the final RMC hut) on a trail far below. Unless you're desperate for shelter, bypass a track that makes this steep descent, saving the Perch for your return.

A welter of trails come and go in this high alpine region where cairns guide your footsteps over telltale boot-marks worn into boulder paths. After the Randolph Path angles upward joining you from the right, the Israel Ridge Trail enters from the same direction, and the routes continue in common for only a few hundred yards. When Israel Ridge diverges left to the top of Mount Adams, bear right on the Randolph Path, which wobbles from cairn to cairn as it finishes the last 0.6 mile to windswept Edmands Col.

A rough connecting bridge between Mount Jefferson and Mount Adams, Edmands Col is a major White Mountain crossroads high above Jefferson Ravine and the Ravine of the Castles, which flank it on either side. From signposts near a patch of ground in this wild central junction, hikers are free to strike out on varied explorations. In less than an hour you'll be awed by views from the top of Mount Adams, begin a return by descending Mount Adams on a section of Lowe's Path, or press beyond the Adams summit on the way to Madison Spring. In 40 minutes you can stand on Jefferson's peak and treat yourself to tantalizing views of the northeast's highest mountain beyond the Great Gulf chasm. Hike a circle of trails that loop over Jefferson's summit, or skirt the absolute top and wander about Monticello Lawn, an elevated wonderland of boulders and rare flowers that blanket the broad expanse of Jefferson's southern flank. Of course you can also be happy just relaxing in the col, staring at clouds nipping at looming summits, scanning the Jefferson highlands, or looking east to the sweep of the Carter Range, which carries the Appalachian Trail all the way to Maine on the far side of Pinkham Notch.

If you're not heading back to Gray Knob or Crag Camp, the Randolph Path makes an easy route of return. As you backtrack out of the col, simply stay on the Randolph Path where the Gray Knob Trail turns right.

This steady, straight, uneventful descent also passes the Perch, the final and least alluring of the four Randolph camps. A crude Adirondack shelter, the Perch provides a fire ring and keeps you out of the rain, but it's also located on a simple trail that leads quickly into the trees. In bad weather, it's good to know it's there.

Remember that after dropping in elevation, the Randolph Path bears east and doesn't return to your original trailhead. Turn left onto Lowe's Path just above the Log Cabin.

Edmands Col and the summit of Mount Adams

The practical guide

Access: From the junction of U.S. Highways 3 and 302 in Twin Mountain, drive 2.0 miles north on Highway 3 and then turn right onto New Hampshire Highway 115. Highway 115 ends at U.S. Highway 2 after about 10 miles. Turn right at the T at Highway 2 and drive 5.0 miles east. The Lowe's Path trailhead is on the south side of the highway just before the Lowe's store and gas station on the opposite side of the road. Park in the Lowe's store gravel lot for a small daily fee.

Accommodations and reservations: All Randolph Mountain Club huts operate on a first-come, first-served basis. Reservations are not accepted, but space is generally available. As of 1997, rates at Gray Knob and Crag Camp are $8/person/night; at the Log Cabin and Perch, $5/person/night. A caretaker is on duty at Crag Camp in July and August and year-round at Gray Knob. Gas stoves are available for use while the caretaker is on duty; at other times, and at other camps, you'll have to bring your own. Always bring food, pots, pans, utensils, sleeping bag, and personal gear. Cold water is available, but needs to be boiled or treated.

Maps: USGS Mount Washington 7.5 x 15; a map of the Randolph Valley & Northern Peaks of the Mount Washington Range is available for $3 from the Randolph Mountain Club at the address below.

For further information: Randolph Mountain Club, Randolph, NH 03570; Androscoggin Ranger District, 80 Glen Road, Gorham, NH 03581, Tel. (603) 466-2713.

15. GRAY KNOB AND CRAG CAMP

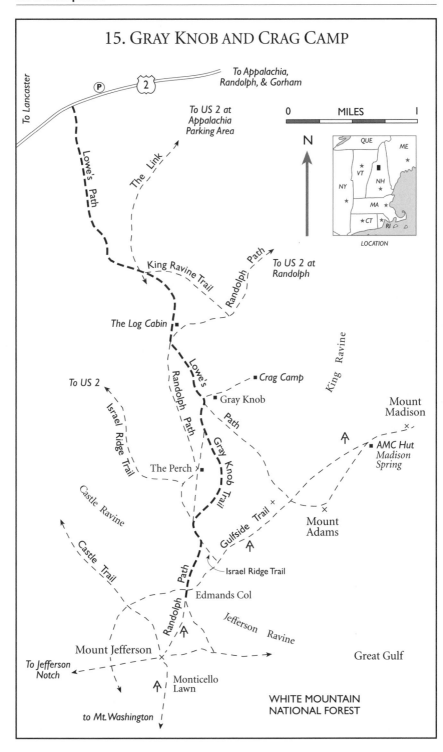

To Lancaster

To Appalachia, Randolph, & Gorham

P 2

To US 2 at Appalachia Parking Area

0 MILES 1

N

LOCATION

QUE
ME
VT
NY
NH
MA
CT
RI

Lowe's Path

The Link

King Ravine Trail

Randolph Path

To US 2 at Randolph

The Log Cabin

King Ravine

Crag Camp

Gray Knob

Lowe's Path

Randolph Path

To US 2

Israel Ridge Trail

Gray Knob Trail

Mount Madison

AMC Hut Madison Spring

The Perch

Castle Ravine

Gulfside Trail

Mount Adams

Castle Trail

Israel Ridge Trail

Randolph Path

Edmands Col

Jefferson Ravine

Mount Jefferson

To Jefferson Notch

Monticello Lawn

Great Gulf

to Mt. Washington

WHITE MOUNTAIN NATIONAL FOREST

New Hampshire

16. Guyot Shelter

Pemigewasset Wilderness, New Hampshire

Guyot Shelter at a glance

Destination: A high mountain shelter on the edge of the Pemigewasset Wilderness

Location: The White Mountains of northern New Hampshire, about 9 miles south of Twin Mountain

Access: Gravel road to the trailhead; hiking trail to the shelter

Difficulty: Rough

Accommodations: Rustic log shelter

Duration: Two or three days

Featured attractions: Breathtaking views from remote wilderness peaks

Picture a really big lima bean — a bean so huge that it covers more than 45,000 acres. Set its rounded bottom facing south just above the Kancamagus Highway, and streak its surface with brooks and rivers that cascade to the west. Rim its top and sides with mountains, Garfield, Zealand, Franconia Ridge, Twin Mountain and the Willey Range — vast mountains that sweep in an arch for more than 30 miles. String the Appalachian Trail along its northern lobes, and right where the bean might sprout, plunk a log shelter on the side of a mountain with glorious daybreak views. Picture the Pemigewasset Wilderness, a White Mountain backcountry treat.

Shielded by mountains from the natural corridors of Crawford Notch and Franconia Notch, this immense basin at the heart of White Mountain National Forest has long been considered remote, one of the largest roadless areas in the eastern United States. Day-trip hikers climb in droves to the edge of this expanse on spectacular Franconia Ridge, while backpackers are more likely to enter from the south following the Lincoln Woods and Wilderness trails on multiple-day excursions that weave beside woodland streams. Less visited are the isolated mountains of the Pemigewasset's northern fringe, where a soaring cliff, a bony peak, and a rounded, rock-strewn summit form a sensational triumvirate. Collectively called "The Bonds" these magnificent peaks sprout from the very core of this preserve, perfectly positioned for visits by hikers who commute from the Guyot Shelter.

Because it was designated a wilderness in 1984 under the provision of the Wilderness Act, a variety of regulations protect the Pemigewasset. A popular haven for backpackers of diverse abilities and experience, this spacious forest will never be "improved" to cater to creature comforts. Group size is limited, mechanical equipment is prohibited, and most existing cabins and shelters are destined to be removed. Thanks to a thoughtful gerrymander, though, the Guyot Shelter will continue to serve long-distance hikers on the neighboring Appalachian Trail and to accommodate intrepid hikers who want to visit the Bonds. Preserved in a special alcove just outside the wilderness zone, Guyot enjoys the best of both hiking worlds — convenient comfort virtually surrounded by permanently protected land.

While not as demanding as the Presidential Peaks, these outlying summits feature a similar essence of unrefined terrain. The same coarse topography that kept loggers at bay until the end of the 19th century makes the Bonds a genuine trek, a far-flung destination where casual hikers are rarely seen. Plan for a long approach, and remember that comfort in these rugged mountains is strictly a relative term. A level floor, a solid roof, a refreshing potable spring, a fire ring, a porch with a view, and a short path to the outhouse door constitute luxury in remote alpine zones. Measured by backcountry standards, Guyot is a four-star stop.

Several paths approach the Guyot Shelter. One route climbs the western slopes of South Twin Mountain, tracking the Appalachian Trail over one of the most gruelling miles of hiking in New Hampshire, while another begins at the Kancamagus Highway and requires a complete traverse of the Pemigewasset Wilderness. Hikers with a focus on comfort should select in-

Guyot Shelter

stead the popular Twinway Trail, which begins near Zealand Notch. This varied, moderate approach allows a night of acclimation at a convenient AMC hut, cuts three miles off the start of your second day of hiking, and makes a logical extension of a trip to Zealand Falls. (See Chapter 21 for directions to the Hut at Zealand Falls)

Angling uphill between the Zealand Hut and cascades feeding Zealand Falls, the Twinway Trail begins the 3.9-mile stretch to Guyot Shelter. Passing the junction with the Lend-A-Hand Trail and crossing a slick-rock stream, hikers who assume the trip will be easy haven't grasped the challenge of wild terrain. Competent hikers will take at least four hours to complete this outbound link without stopping for food or views. Plan five or six hours to really enjoy your day.

The eastern slopes of Zealand Ridge are the toughest climb of the day as the trail slabs through a hardwood forest on the way to the level top of this long mountain ridge. Surrounded by shrubs and shadowed by distant peaks, a well-worn path adds about 100 yards to your hike before your arrival at Zeacliff Junction. Wander left on this short detour to an outcrop with majestic views. As you share a cliff-side boulder with a hungry Canada jay, lustrous shards of Whitewall Mountain seem to plunge into Zealand Notch, Ethan Pond hides in the woods just west of the Willey Range, and the untamed summits of the Pemigewasset Wilderness ramble to the east.

After you pass Zeacliff Junction, the next 0.75 mile is an easy jaunt along the crest of Zealand Ridge, a gradual westward ascent on a sometimes muddy track that dips beneath evergreens. Another spur descends 0.1 mile to the left (south) to reach Zeacliff Pond, a snug pool where a family of ducks is part of the mountainous scene.

Boulder steps and a split-log ladder aid the ascent of a ragged knoll just beyond the spur to Zeacliff Pond, as the Twinway bobs and weaves along a suddenly knobby ridge. Passing 4000 feet, the trail steadies again and rolls so gradually to the top of Zealand Mountain that the side path to its highest point would not be seen without a sign. Beyond the summit, a steep descent grants only partial views of Guyot Mountain's eastern slopes as the Twinway bottoms out and resumes a gradual climb of Guyot's double-top windblown peak.

Sheltering conifers slowly yield to a krummholz-laden knob on the north peak of Guyot Mountain. Pick your way carefully off the trail through openings in the knee-high growth, stepping only on rocky shards that share this rounded summit with delicate vegetation. This highest point on Guyot Mountain is less inviting than the nearby southern peak, but a short stop on these alpine heights still grants a marvelous view of Mount Washington as it dominates the Presidential Range.

New Hampshire

Zeacliff views of the snow-capped Mount Washington Range

Follow the cairns over the knob to the Bondcliff Trail and bear left (south) at this junction one mile from the Guyot Shelter. A brief dip through protective trees rises again to picturesque South Peak, where a large cairn and a spacious top bid hikers to relax. The silence here is so intense that rumbling rocks snap your attention to a slide on a distant peak. Mosses, lichens, and scattered rocks provide a typical alpine environment, as wilderness peaks in all directions are too numerous to be counted.

Sunny days make exposed summits exceptional attractions, but the Bondcliff Trail wisely retreats below treeline before reaching a protected path to year-round accommodations. At the low point of a ridge about half way between Guyot's South Peak and the summit of Mount Bond, a dead-end spur turns east 0.2 mile to the Guyot Shelter. About 250 vertical feet below, a caretaker's tent, pit toilet, tent platforms, and reliable spring rest on the side of a hill near a double-decker, peeled-log shelter that overlooks mountain and valley. Bring a sleeping bag and a foam pad to share the layered decks designed for up to twelve hikers, and pack a stove to prepare meals with views from the covered porch.

Deep in the mountains far from any trailhead, Guyot Shelter offers the only practical way to enjoy whole days of wandering throughout the fabulous Bonds. Retrace your steps back up the spur to the junction with the Bondcliff Trail, and find yourself within striking distance of three phenomenal mountains. Want a pinnacled peak with jagged boulders reaching to the sky? Turn south on the Bondcliff Trail, enter the Pemigewasset Wilderness, and climb just 0.2 mile to another spur that scrambles to West Bond's point. Want a massive mountain with alpine flowers blooming across its peak? Continue south on the Bondcliff Trail to complete the next half mile, which rises to Mount Bond's summit and majestic alpine heights. Want a knife-edge trail with soaring cliffs vanishing beneath your feet? Persist on a southern course, plunge through boulders at Mount Bond's feet, and trace the edge of a precipice to amazing Bondcliff sights.

As distinctive as each of the summits in the Bonds may be, they all enjoy common world-class views. Virtually surrounded by a wilderness zone showing no trace of human intrusion, panoramas from these extraordinary peaks challenge your sense of adventure. Mounts Lafayette, Lincoln, Liberty, and Flume grandly rise from north to south on inviting Franconia Ridge, while Franconia Brook deftly falls through miles of appealing forest and joins the East Branch of the Pemigewasset River as it makes its way to the sea. All around, mountains fall in graceful arches to streams on valley floors, or plunge in bare-gashed rock slides to the bottom of an angled notch. Immersed in the heart of a wilderness basin visited only by kindred spirits, hikers have reason enough to consider the Bonds their favorite White Mountain peaks.

The practical guide

Access: Zealand Road runs south from US Highway 302 2.1 miles east of the junction of US Highways 3 and 302 in Twin Mountain. After passing through a Forest Service Campground, Zealand Road dead-ends at a large parking area at the Zealand trailhead, 3.4 miles from the highway. Hike the Zealand Trail 2.5 miles to the Twinway and Ethan Pond junction near the south end of Zealand Pond, and then follow the Twinway

Trail 0.2 mile uphill to the Zealand Hut, where the Guyot hike begins.

Accommodations and reservations: Guyot Shelter operates on a first-come, first-served basis. Reservations are not accepted. A fee is collected to defray operating costs during the summer when a caretaker is on duty.

Maps: USGS South Twin Mountain and Crawford Notch quads; See also the AMC "Franconia" map.

For further information: Ammonoosuc Ranger Station, Box 239, Bethlehem, NH 03574, Tel. (603) 869-2626.

New Hampshire

16. GUYOT SHELTER

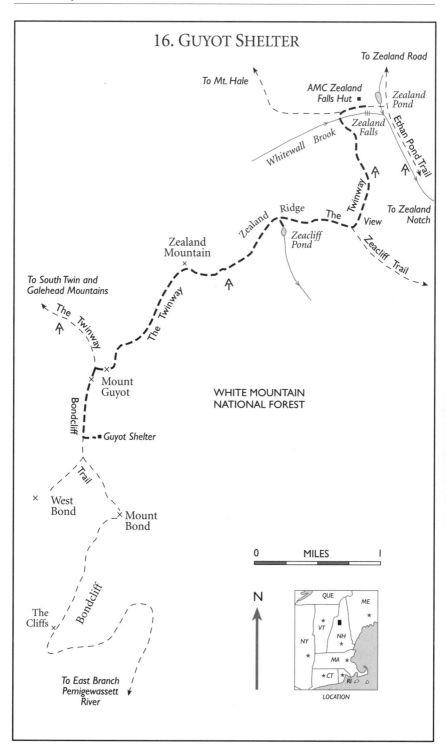

To Zealand Road

To Mt. Hale

AMC Zealand
Falls Hut

Zealand
Pond

Zealand
Falls

Whitewall Brook

Ethan Pond Trail

Twinway

Zealand Ridge

The

View

To Zealand
Notch

Zealand
Mountain

Zeacliff
Pond

Zeacliff Trail

To South Twin and
Galehead Mountains

The Twinway

The Twinway

The Twinway

Bondcliff

Mount
Guyot

Guyot Shelter

WHITE MOUNTAIN
NATIONAL FOREST

Trail

West
Bond

Mount
Bond

Bondcliff

The
Cliffs

To East Branch
Pemigewassett
River

0   MILES   1

N

LOCATION

QUE

ME

VT

NH

NY

MA

CT

RI

New Hampshire

17. The Hut at Madison Spring
White Mountains, New Hampshire

Madison Spring at a glance

Destination: Stone hut in the Presidential Peaks
Location: Northern New Hampshire, about 8 miles west of Gorham
Access: Car or shuttle bus to the trailhead; hiking trail to the hut
Difficulty: Rough
Accommodations: Shared bunkrooms in a mountain hut
Duration: Two or three days
Featured attractions: Nights above timberline and stunning White Mountain views

Stone cairns lost in passing clouds, majestic summit views, plummeting headwalls, steep ravines, and broad mountain shoulders speckled with alpine flowers. Little wonder that the Presidential Peaks in the White Mountains of New Hampshire represent the best in New England hiking. Each year, more than 1200 miles of trails and 20 developed campgrounds in the 770,000-acre White Mountain National Forest draw more visitors to the northern tier of the granite state than go to Yellowstone National Park. Dominating the core of a vast wilderness of recreational delights, the summits of Mounts Washington, Adams, Jefferson, Monroe and Madison stand as a dignified group, the five highest peaks in the northeastern United States and, not so coincidentally, home of the worst weather in America.

An extreme climate no doubt explains why stout huts of stone and timber have existed at Madison Spring since 1888. Temperatures on nearby Mount Washington have never exceeded 72 degrees, and gale force winds have been know to top 230 miles per hour. In the Presidential Peaks, strong winds, 40 degree readings, driving rains, and thunderstorms occur throughout the summer, and conditions change at the drop of a hat. But a fragile alpine environment, not inclement weather, is the real reason that (in the summer) Forest Service regulations limit overnight stays above timberline to a hut. On mountaintops covered by alpine plants normally at home in arctic regions a thousand miles further north, the backpacker's limitation becomes the average hiker's golden chance. Let clouds fly and darkness fall, visitors to Madison Spring rest comfortably beneath wool blankets snug in a protected bunk, with congenial meals to end their day, get them started, or warm them up.

Hunkered in a rocky col between Mount Madison's summit cone and multiple-peaked Mount Adams, Madison is the northernmost of the eight backcountry huts maintained by the Appalachian Mountain Club (AMC), a 120-year-old association of hikers and conservationists that welcomes the general public to its huts. Located a day's hike apart along mountainous portions of the Appalachian Trail, the AMC huts of the White Mountains are far from the rustic hovels that their name may first imply.

New Hampshire

Accommodating about 50 guests in two large bunk rooms, with restrooms, gaslit sitting/dining area, spacious kitchen, and crew's quarters, all set amidst the finest scenery in the eastern United States, Madison Spring is a classic White Mountain hut. Staffed by "croos" who cook family-style meals, relay weather forecasts, answer a thousand questions, and pack all the food you'll eat up the mountain, huts are safe, convenient havens, blessed with the luxury of alpine sunsets that transform the highest peaks into vivid mountain scenes.

Several trails converge on Madison Spring. For the safest, least stressful route, plan on ascending the Valley Way, a protected path that avoids alpine exposure until arrival at the hut. Though moderate and direct, the Valley Way resists a boring label. Tracking the course of Snyder Brook as it tumbles from its watershed, the route crosses varied paths to small cascades and waterfalls, including a convenient 0.1 mile detour onto the Fallsway loop about halfway into the hike. Fact is, there's no easy way to gain 3500 feet without putting one foot in front of the other, but this honorable path distracts you with views as the climb begins to get steep. Take your time, drink plenty of water, and rest often to enjoy the scene as the trail ascends a narrowing ravine cut into Mount Madison's flank. People of all ages and levels of conditioning successfully complete this hike. The effort is never as difficult as the towering mountain makes it seem. When you pass a spur on the right that leads to tent platforms designed for hardy backpackers, you'll know you've begun the rocky assault on the last half mile of the hike.

Mount Madison and the hut at Madison Spring

A traditional structure of stone lined in the deep honey color of pine with long experience, the hut at Madison Spring rests just above timberline at 4800 feet, a destination that's truly special. Edged by krummholz and stunted firs, the hut emerges from the mists of a rocky col, just a quarter mile from the most breathtaking panorama that can be found in all the White Mountains. Enter the great room, settle your pack, warm up with a hot drink, and before long you'll be off exploring this alpine realm unencumbered by cares about cooking meals or pitching a tent. Just be sure to synchronize your watch to make it back to the hut for dinner.

A superb day of hiking could be spent within a mile of Madison Spring. Bear east if you like, on the Osgood Trail for an easy 30-minute jaunt up the pile of rocks behind the hut. This casual climb ends on Mount Madison's dazzling peak with endless views of lesser mountains and a glimpse of the evening sun. If time and energy are ample, set off instead on the opposite tack for the rough and rugged one-mile climb to Mount Adams' mystical height, a one-hour scramble that lands you atop New England's second highest peak.

Visitors will be happy to discover, though, that the finest scenery in the Presidential Peaks can be reached from Madison Hut with little additional effort. Head south on the Star Lake and Parapet trails, gently rising over stony terrain where mosses, lichens, labrador tea, mountain cranberries, small azaleas, and vast collections of alpine flowers beautifully survive in the harsh environment of a windswept col. Within 0.2 mile you'll reach the frigid waters of Star Lake, reflecting Mount Adams' peak on the face of its tiny pool. A few paces more deliver hikers to the stunning Parapet, a sheer precipice of boulders at the very brink of the White Mountain world.

While you're poised on the Parapet's lip, the immense flanks of the giant mountains that stand to your left and right plunge with stark finality into the emptiness of space. Madison Gulf and Jefferson Ravine open beneath your feet, vast chasms that add small measure to the gaping abyss of the enormous Great Gulf. Miles across this broad expanse, a ribbon of road snakes to the top of Mount Washington's eastern ridge, and the distant summits of the Carter Range serve as ragged backdrops for miniature ski slopes in Pinkham Notch. A superlative viewpoint that never disappoints, this splendid outcrop might inspire first-time visitors to make this hike an annual event.

Experienced trekkers may be intrigued by a popular extension of the Valley Way hike that links a stay at Madison Spring with additional days in the Presidential Peaks. Typical excursions traverse the range and descend to Pinkham Notch or spend a second night at Lakes-of-the-Clouds hut south of Mount Washington's peak. In good weather it's a wonderful hike; in bad weather, full of hazard. Be certain of your conditioning, carry maps and adequate equipment, consult specialized guides, and check with local sources before attempting an extended hike.

Hiking around Star Lake below Mount Madison's peak

The practical guide

Access: To find the Valley Way Trail, drive north on New Hampshire Highway 16 through Pinkham Notch and turn west onto U.S. Highway 2 in the town of Gorham. The well-marked Appalachia parking lot is on the south side of the road, about 6 miles west of town. Signs are posted at the trailhead, and the 3.8-mile Valley Way is clearly blazed all the way to the hut.

The Appalachia parking lot is also a stop on the AMC hikers shuttle, a van service that links Pinkham Notch (the AMC Visitors Center) and several popular trailheads. Fees are modest and schedules are posted. Reservations are possible though generally not required except on weekends. Whether you leave your vehicle at the Appalachia lot or at Pinkham Notch on the opposite side of the mountain, the shuttle service gives hikers the freedom to follow their whims or the dictates of changeable weather.

Accommodations and reservations: For reservations only, call the Appalachian Mountain Club in Pinkham Notch at (603) 466-2727. The Madison and Lakes-of-the-Clouds huts are open only from early June to mid-September, but huts at lower elevations extend the season well into Fall and Spring. Two popular huts are even open all year. Contact the AMC for seasonal rates and self-service options that are offered in less active months.

Maps: USGS Mount Washington 7.5 x 15; also the Appalachian Mountain Club map of the Mount Washington Range, available from the address below or at the visitors center in Pinkham Notch.

For further information: Appalachian Mountain Club, 5 Joy Street, Boston, MA 02108 or Appalachian Mountain Club, Pinkham Notch Visitor Center, Box 298, Gorham, NH 03581; Also Androscoggin Ranger District, 80 Glen Road, Gorham, NH, 03581, Tel. (603) 466-2713.

New Hampshire

17. THE HUT AT MADISON SPRING

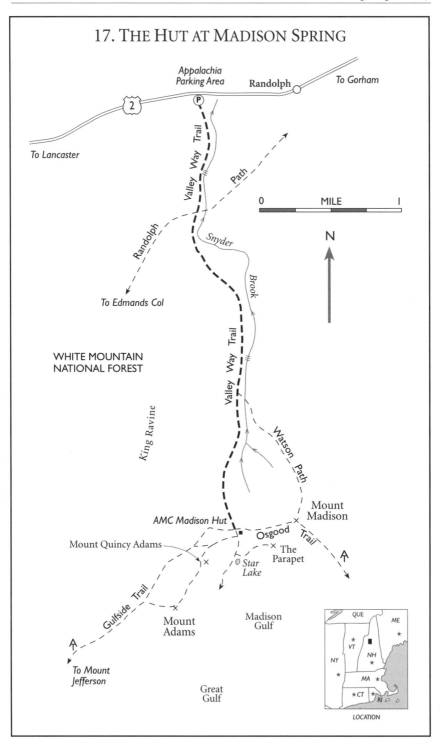

To Lancaster

2

Appalachia
Parking Area   Randolph   To Gorham

Valley Way Trail

Path

0   MILE   1

N

Randolph

Snyder

Brook

To Edmands Col

WHITE MOUNTAIN
NATIONAL FOREST

Valley Way Trail

King Ravine

Watson Path

Mount
Madison

AMC Madison Hut

Osgood Trail

Mount Quincy Adams

The
Parapet

Star
Lake

Gulfside Trail

Mount
Adams

Madison
Gulf

To Mount
Jefferson

Great
Gulf

LOCATION

QUE
ME
VT
NH
NY
MA
CT
RI

18. The Monadnock Region
Jaffrey and Fitzwilliam, New Hampshire

Monadnock at a glance

Destination: Classic country inns of Currier and Ives New England
Location: In the southwest corner of New Hampshire, about 12 miles from
   Keene
Access: Bike or drive a circular tour of trailheads and historic sites
Difficulty: Easy to Moderate
Accommodations: Comfortable to very comfortable
Duration: Weekend or overnight
Featured attractions: Mount Monadnock, Rhododendron State Park, and
   historic southern New Hampshire

Twelve thousand years ago, rock and gravel captured in mile-thick ice
pummeled the New England landscape. Glacial tongues scraped and
gouged, pushing inexorably south, plucking boulders from mountaintops
and scouring contoured valleys. A few bold peaks defied the devastation.
Polished and ground, Mount Monadnock's bare cone, still wearing the
striated scars, stands today as the textbook definition of a mountain of
resistant rock.

This isolated peak rising east of the Connecticut Valley lends its
name to this section of rural New Hampshire, but other remnants of the
Ice Age give the region its distinctive look. Drumlins (hill-sized mounds of
glacial deposits) and kettle holes (water-filled gaps in glacial debris) form
a cordial landscape of gently rolling terrain pockmarked in random patterns by shallow lakes and tranquil ponds. Winding roads and quiet villages enhance these pastoral scenes, which long ago inspired the artistry
of Currier and Ives.

Civilization displaced wilderness in this vicinity more than 200 years
ago, and Mount Monadnock currently ranks among the most frequently
climbed summits in the world. Yet in spite of the crowds and bustling
towns there is beauty to be found, and a primary source of a portion of
America's heritage. On the well-worn paths of Monadnock's slopes, in the
soaring summit views, among wildflowers gathered on nature trails, and
in the symmetry of clapboard homes lurks the very inspiration shared by
Emerson and Thoreau. While biking and touring the Monadnock region,
you'll savor picturesque scenes, and perhaps find a link to the naturalist
tradition at the core of New England life.

You don't have to bike this twenty-mile circuit to get to the heart of
the matter. Visitors put off by a few stiff hills or busy country roads may
be quite content to drive this easy loop, but the horse-and-buggy speeds
of a bicycle tour set a much more suitable pace. Stop for a glimpse of
Mount Monadnock beyond an apple grove. Lounge on the lawn of a meet-

inghouse framed by autumn leaves, or just pause as clouds float over a steeple high in the crisp blue sky.

Whatever your means of locomotion, a choice selection of well-placed inns allows guests to start a tour at any of several points along this route. Begin and end at one location for a quick one-day spin, or link two or three inns on succeeding nights for a delightful weekend stay. I began at the Fitzwilliam Inn, a renowned lodging with 25 rooms, fine dining, and a cozy pub, admirably serving the wayfaring public since 1796. With a rocking-chair porch comfortably surveying the library, church, and stately dwellings that share the Fitzwilliam common, its a grand spot to slowly absorb a first taste of Monadnock history.

To assure an easygoing rhythm, start your tour with a short excursion in the opposite direction. From the head of the town common, follow Richmond Road past the side door of the Fitzwilliam Inn and turn right onto Rhododendron Road after only 0.7 mile. Less than two miles later, the pavement ends at Rhododendron State Park, a National Natural Landmark that charms visitors with gentle trails winding through a veritable jungle of native rhododendron. Wayside benches surrounded by blooms and a shaded picnic ground encourage a proper pace in the State of New Hampshire's only designated botanic site. Fifteen acres of arching shrubs burst with blossoms in mid-July, but a wildflower trail maintained by the local garden club educates amateur naturalists with samples of native plants throughout the summer.

Backtrack to the Fitzwilliam Inn and you're ready to pedal toward Jaffrey on the southern leg of your tour. Steer directly across the head of the com-

The historic Fitzwilliam Inn

mon past a market and Rainy Day books, and coast 0.25 mile from the village green to a junction with Highway 12. Use caution as you aim straight across this busy high-speed road and ride east on Highway 119, following signs toward the Town of Rindge. The first two miles will test your mettle. There's not much to look at, and one of the stiffest hill climbs on the loop, but a roadside barn, a stone wall, and a cluster of paper birch that share views at the top of a ridge soon mark the scenic start of your rural Monadnock journey. Beyond Fullam Hill Road, the rest of the 4.6-mile stretch on Highway 119 is mostly an easy glide past duck-filled marshes and the breezy shores of kettle-hole Pearly Pond. Turn left at a blinking light into the entrance to Franklin Pierce College, an easy pedaling access road leading past sandy beaches and athletic fields that meld in a college scene. A homecoming band or a soccer game might offer a brief diversion before bikers turn right near the top of a hill at a stop sign on the edge of campus.

Peace and quiet reign after a short, steep climb on newly paved Mountain Road, which twists and turns through placid woods with plenty of gear shifts up and down. This 1.6-mile backdoor entrance to the college pauses at Pool Pond before passing a church and ending at the side of US Highway 202. Turn left (north) for an 0.9-mile leg on this major thoroughfare, which is luckily endowed with broad shoulders, keeping cyclists away from traffic. Near the north end of the lake that flanks the highway on the left, turn right for a brief stint on Davis Crossing Road. Just after the turn, a 100-yard detour on an abandoned railroad bed leads to a private overlook in the Contoocook Marsh Recreation Area, before riders return to the route, skirting the wetlands on Davis Crossing Road and turning left onto Woodbound Road after 0.2 mile. A rolling excursion on a quiet road, this 1.7-mile link passes dense woods and shaded homes bordering Contoocook Lake as it curls through pines and weaves its way to the welcoming Woodbound Inn.

A large lodge by New England standards, the Woodbound Inn appears less intimate than other options, but par-three golf, a sandy beach, a tennis court, and a resort-style activity center make this lakeside stop a nice choice for extended stays and for families with active children. A fireplace in the parlor, a wood-beamed dining room, modern units, and private lake-front cabins combine with 15 kilometers of cross-country ski trails to offer year-round accommodations.

Only 2.5 miles, a community beach, and a small-town residential area separate the Woodbound Inn from the center of Jaffrey. Continue north on Woodbound Road and bear left at the ⊤ at Squantum Road. Pass the sand beach, stay on Squantum Road at the fork with Howard Hill, turn right onto Stratton Road at a stop sign by a park, and you'll quickly arrive at traffic lights in the commercial center of Jaffrey. Turn left on Highway 124 and walk your bike down Main Street of this historic manufacturing town. Amble along the sidewalk, buy refreshments from local shops, and admire the beauty of the recycled mills that line a raceway on the Contoocook River.

History and nature mingle on the northern half of the Monadnock circuit, which arches west from the middle of Jaffrey. Passing the civic center and gazebo on the old-time village green, Highway 124 rises steadily out of town lined by trees, churches and New England homes that have stood for generations. Whiffs of woodsmoke set the mood for the next 1.8 miles as bikers pedal from 19th century brick-milled Jaffrey to 17th century Jaffrey Center, site of the town's earliest settlement. The gleaming symmetry of the clapboard homes in this charming wayside cluster preserves the architectural splendor of the region's village past. Strategically placed by the side of the road in the center of this historic village, the Monadnock Inn purveys an intimate atmosphere. Traditional New England rooms, fine dining, and a popular Sunday brunch make this genteel inn a comfortable favorite, convenient to Mount Monadnock and the wealth of cultural attractions that flourish in the region.

Climbing another hill on the way out of Jaffrey Center, a slight digression onto Meetinghouse Road leads to one of the most beautiful man-made structures in southern New Hampshire. With a clock tower, classic lines, and rows of stately windows, the Old Jaffrey Meeting House is a fine place to enjoy a summer concert or marvel at its autumn beauty when framed by golden maples.

Heading west from the meetinghouse on Highway 124, a 0.25-mile glide brings bikers to Dublin Road and a sign for Monadnock State Park. If hiking is on your agenda, travel north 1.3 miles on Dublin Road to the park entrance and the most popular Monadnock trailhead. A rustic shelter, nature center, and log hikers cabin welcome visitors of all ages to the base of this historic mountain, which evokes the respected heritage of New England naturalist tradition. Well-trod paths lead up the wooded slopes to Emerson's Seat, Thoreau's Seat, the Sarcophagus and a host of geographic features that reflect Monadnock's storied past.

Bicyclists with stout footwear, a day pack, and three or four hours to spare can hike to the top of this prominent mountain for terrific summit views. The moderate White Dot and White Cross trails diverge about 0.5

Scanning three-state horizons from the top of Mount Monadnock

mile beyond the trailhead and reunite on the upper heights, surrounded by labrador tea, blueberries, and windblown birch in the shadow of the looming peak. Both trails scale the faces of scarified granite that form the summit's cone, a smooth rock scramble that ends on a craggy top with stupendous views and hidden crannies that delight adventurous kids. Massachusetts, Vermont, and New Hampshire summits are visible from this isolated perch while closer at hand a full panorama of fields, forests, hillocks, and pools define the Monadnock Region.

The last stage of the Monadnock tour returns to Highway 124 for a final ride through the rumpled landscape that was seen from the mountaintop. A hard pedal up a long hill ends with a coasting descent and a left turn onto Fitzwilliam Road, where a classic glimpse of Mount Monadnock emerges on the right. Civilization quickly fades into country scenes in these final 4.2 miles, which recall the fabled images of New England of yesteryear. Sheep, hayfields, and colonial farms mingle with pungent woods on this roller-coaster ride that serves as a fitting climax to a rural New Hampshire trip. A quick downhill burst brings bikers back to the present at a junction with Highway 12. Cross the road and proceed less than 100 yards. To your right is the head of the common, the familiar Fitzwilliam Inn, and the sudden end of your tour.

The practical guide

Access: The Monadnock Region wouldn't be special if it weren't a trifle hard to reach. Highway 101 between Keene and the greater Manchester/Nashua area is the primary access route. From east or west, follow Highway 101 to Peterborough and then turn south on US Highway 202, which leads to the Town of Jaffrey. From the Keene area, Highway 12 provides a more direct route to the Fitzwilliam end of the tour.

Accommodations and reservations: The Fitzwilliam Inn, Route 119, Fitzwilliam, NH 03447, Tel. (603) 585-9000; The Monadnock Inn, 379 Main Street, Jaffrey, NH 03452, Tel. (603) 532-7001; The Woodbound Inn, Rindge, NH 03461, Tel. (603) 532-8341. Advance reservations are always advised.

Maps: State of New Hampshire highway maps portray the major roads; for hiking on Mount Monadnock, see USGS Monadnock Mountain 7.5 X 15, or handout map of the "Main Trails of Mt. Monadnock," available at the park entrance or from the state park address below; for Rhododendron State Park, obtain a map and brochure from Rhododendron State Park at the address below.

For further information: Monadnock State Park, P.O. Box 181, Jaffrey, NH 03452-0181, Tel. (603) 532-8862; Rhododendron State Park, P.O. Box 181, Jaffrey, NH 03452-0181, Tel. (603) 532-8862.

18. The Monadnock Region

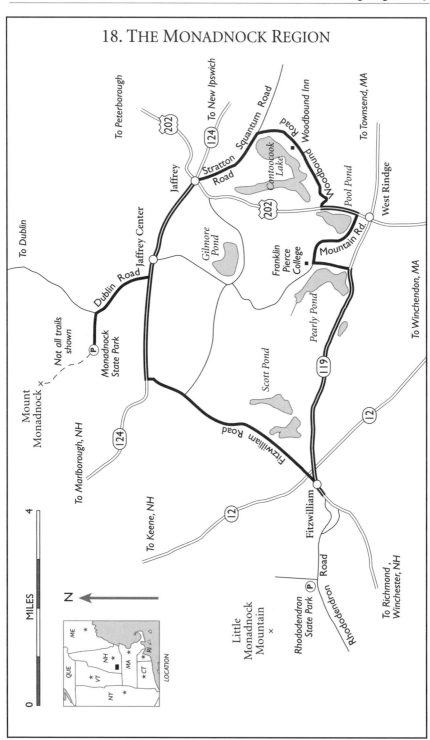

19. Phillips Brook Backcountry Recreation Area

White Mountains, New Hampshire

Phillips Brook at a glance

Destination: An experimental center for backcountry recreation in a private New Hampshire forest.

Location: North of the White Mountain National Forest, between Berlin and Colebrook, New Hampshire

Access: Gravel road to the trailhead; bike, hike, ski, or drive to varied accommodations

Difficulty: Moderate; Easy if driving to lodge

Accommodations: Comfortable lake-front lodge or heated yurts and cabins

Duration: From two nights to as long as you please

Featured attractions: Backcountry travel from hut to hut or excursions from a classic lodge.

Phillips Brook occupies one of those untracked regions that highway maps cover with a compass rose, an undeveloped part of the state where roads just never go. Even further north than the northern lobe of White Mountain National Forest, only game trails and logging routes penetrate this timberland. Ignored at present by the mass of hikers who journey to the Presidential Peaks 20 miles to the south, this 24,000-acre watershed now plays a central role in an innovative experiment in backcountry recreation.

The first facility of its kind in the eastern United States, the Phillips Brook Recreation Area is a visionary effort to establish a profitable business by offering hut-to-hut backcountry lodging on privately owned land. In a year when the United States Forest Service has imposed an annual fee for walking in the White Mountains, the timing may be right for this creative enterprise that welcomes hiking, biking, skiing, and fishing, but charges only for overnight use. Operated by Timberland Trails, Inc. on land leased from International Paper Company, Phillips Brook remains a work in progress and a test of whether commercial logging and recreation can happily coexist.

Separated from the 45,000-acre Nash Stream State Forest by the crest of a mountain ridge, Phillips Brook flows north to south through an enormous watershed that's crosshatched by smaller streams and valleys. While Nash Stream shows the effects of abuse by former owners, this high-quality hardwood forest managed by International Paper for the past 100 years is a welcome study in contrast. Even during a harvest, it's hard to tell where trees have been cut on these densely timbered slopes. No clear cuts or graded banks mar the wild woodlands that surround Phillips

Phillips Brook near Paris Field Base

Brook, where a picture-perfect trout stream flows through a graceful valley. A system of separate trails, a geography that assures that recreational users don't share locations with loggers, and a friendly escort for vehicles that are headed to the lodge, means most visitors enjoy a quiet setting and never sense that this wilderness is also a working forest.

From a waterfall over rugged rocks near the entrance at Paris Base to the peaceful home of haunting loons on a beautiful mountain lake, there's much to discover at Phillips Brook, with unique forms of overnight shelter to help you enjoy your stay. Be ready for an experience, though, more adventurous than you might expect. In spite of the comfortable quarters, visitors are on their own, and the wilderness is very real. No efforts have been made to tame this land, and many of the old logging paths are overgrown and obscure. ATV's, dirt bikes, and other motorized equipment aren't welcome at Phillips Brook. Instead, bring map, compass, and route-finding skills that will be in great demand.

A two-story lodge overlooking a pond is the centerpiece of Phillips Brook, a classic retreat in the finest backwoods tradition. Four bedrooms (two with private bath), gas heat, electric lights, a dining room, and a complete kitchen afford pleasant surroundings, but the ambiance of this homey cabin makes your stay extraordinary. Cane rockers on a screened porch share views of Phillips Pond, the summit of Whitcomb Mountain, and a grove of paper birch. Maple floors and log walls cast a honey-colored glow over groupings of cushioned chairs, and a six-foot fireplace of handpicked river stones makes the living room warm and toasty. Reserve a single room or the entire building for private groups. The lodge at Phillips Brook is a gracious base for daily wanderings at any time of year.

If hut-to-hut travel is on your mind, you'll likely stay in a yurt. The traditional structure of Mongol nomads has reappeared in the north woods in 20th century form, still round, but made of synthetic material and vented at its peak. As constructed at Phillips Brook, these 20-foot-diam-

Modern-day yurt at Phillips Brook

eter shelters come complete with a wooden deck, individual cots, a gas stove for cooking, and a wood stove for heat. Gentle on the environment, soft-sided yurts place overnight guests in intimate touch with nature, a relationship you'll quickly understand if a coyote brushes the wall of your hut in the middle of the night.

Yurts and cabins are sprinkled throughout the Phillips Brook watershed, all sited with an eye for detail by a landscape architect. A yurt not far from the entrance accommodates late arrivals. A yurt in a col on Long Mountain attracts people who ski the glades, and a yurt at the end of Whitcomb Mountain invites hikers to Trio Ponds. Two log cabins and two additional yurts are located on an elaborate system of woods roads and trails that make hut-to-hut itineraries flexible throughout the year. Future plans are more intriguing. Look for a hostel at Paris Base, an overnight cabin high atop a firetower, and even a tree house or two.

From customized guided group trips to a llama-supported trek, from lazy days watching clouds go by to extended solo hikes, there's no shortage of things to do in any active season. As a possible training ground for dog-sled racing teams, this north-country valley provides enough reliable snow throughout the winter to rival central Quebec. Over 50 miles of woods roads and fresh-cut forest trails carry snowshoers and Nordic skiers across the rolling terrain, or you can climb to the ridge of Long Mountain for the excitement of telemark skiing through wooded hillside glades. When the snows melt, high water turns Phillips Brook into a foaming kayak run before late spring reduces the flow to usher in brook-trout season. In summer and fall, hikers are free to wander unencumbered to lakes and bogs and hillside forests with views from the highest ridges to the summits of the Mahoosuc Range and the Presidential Peaks. For the first time in the East, mountain bikers have miles of roads with access to overnight huts, and anyone can inquire at the entrance for directions to that special spot where a swimming hole in a brisk stream is hidden in a forest glade.

The practical guide

Access: New Hampshire Highway 110 runs east-west between Groveton and Berlin, New Hampshire, as it skims the northern end of White Mountain National Forest. Stark village is located on Highway 110 6.8 miles east of its junction with U.S. Highway 3. Turn north onto Paris Road 4.6 miles east of the covered bridge in the village of Stark. Cross a one-lane bridge over the Upper Ammonoosuc River, pass straight through a four-way intersection, and bear right at a fork 2.1 miles from Highway 110. The Paris Field Base entrance to the Phillips Brook Backcountry Recreation Area is 1.3 miles beyond the fork in the gravel road.

Paris Field Base is the point of departure for day trips or overnight journeys to all of the yurts and cabins. Guests staying at Phillips Brook Lodge may either hike, bike, or ski to Phillips Pond on their own, or drive the final 9 miles with an escort over active logging roads.

Accommodations and reservations: Phillips Brook Recreation Area does not charge for day use of roads and trails, but only for overnight lodging. Reservations and a Waiver and Release form are required for overnight guests. Any cabin, yurt, or lodge can be shared by separate parties or reserved for the exclusive use of a private group. Stove tops, pots and pans, and utensils are supplied. Bring a sleeping bag (or sheets and towels for the lodge), food, personal items, and required backcountry gear.

Maps: USGS Dummer Ponds and Dixville Notch quads; Trail maps are also available at Paris Base.

For further information: Timberland Trails, Inc., P.O. Box 1076, Conway, NH 03818, Tel. (603) 447-1786, 1-800-TRAILS-8.

New Hampshire

20. Lake Umbagog and Lake Umbagog National Wildlife Refuge

Errol, New Hampshire

Umbagog at a glance

Destination: Wilderness campsites on the shore of an unspoiled lake
Location: About 20 miles north of Berlin, on the Maine/New Hampshire border.
Access: Water taxi or private boat
Difficulty: Easy
Accommodations: Secluded campsite at water's edge
Duration: Overnight or extended stay
Featured attractions: Moose, bear, osprey, loons and even a bald eagle on a large wilderness lake

Definitions of "wilderness" are very subjective. Some people demand a virgin forest unscarred by signs of humans. Others include a wooded grove surrounded by a city. Lake Umbagog falls somewhere between these two extremes, but when moose, bear, beaver, loons, osprey, and mergansers visit your camp within a twenty-four hour period, you'll have to admit that this pristine lake deserves the wilderness designation.

A shallow lake extending more than 10 miles along the Maine/New Hampshire border, Lake Umbagog is a throwback to an earlier era. Permanent camps are few, and on any given day, there's a real chance that you'll see more loons than power boats as you paddle these dark waters. A very irregular coast studded with inlets, coves, and bays gives Lake Umbagog more than 50 miles of shore and breaks a large expanse of water into small intimate bits. The same manageable scale that attracts vacationing humans also satisfies the nesting instincts of territorial loons, making Lake Umbagog one of the most productive breeding grounds for these birds in the northeastern United States.

Numerous islands, the largest freshwater marsh complex remaining in New Hampshire, and an undeveloped coast, provide outstanding habitat for waterfowl, rare plants, and endangered and threatened species. As a result, with the cooperation of timber companies, private owners, conservation organizations, and the states of New Hampshire and Maine, the U.S. Fish and Wildlife Service established the Lake Umbagog National Wildlife Refuge in 1992. Spread principally along Umbagog's western shore, this growing refuge preserves and protects through ownership or easement more than seven thousand acres of critical habitat. Wood ducks, Canada geese, warblers, and herons frequent these marshes and shores, while a concentration of nesting osprey gather abundant prey from waters rich with fish. On the lake's northwestern margin, a broad expanse of wetlands near the junction of the Androscoggin and Magalloway rivers forms the centerpiece of the new preserve, where New Hampshire's only nesting pair of bald eagles established a home in recent years. Across the lake, private lands supply another dimension. Rising gently into Maine, unspoiled hills of spruce and fir provide excellent habitat for hidden populations of bobcat, coyote, and fisher as well as larger mammals like moose, deer, and bear that often wander into view.

Remote and largely pristine, this alluring lake is remarkably easy to visit. With water-taxi service to support young families or campers just getting started, a weekend on Lake Umbagog combines easy access with great backcountry camping. Located at the southern end of the lake not far from the Maine border, Umbagog Lake Campground maintains a boat launch,

Bald eagle, Lake Umbagog National Wildlife Refuge

base camp, and several waterfront cabins along with 33 wilderness campsites spread across the lake. While the campground at the base won't appeal to backcountry campers, the wilderness sites that are tucked into coves, hidden on islands, or plunked atop rocky points supply unbeatable enclaves for viewing Umbagog's nature. Ranging from 1 to 11 miles away from the southern base, campers reach the wilderness sites by motor boat, kayak, and canoe, or elect to ride on a pontoon boat that serves as a water taxi ferrying parties and all of their gear to and from a camp. One-way fees vary with the distance of your campsite from the base. Even for experienced paddlers, the service is worth the price, especially when winds kick up waves on this fickle northern lake.

All sites have private frontage, plenty of space, a picnic table, a pit toilet, and a stone fire ring, and wildlife can always be seen from any camp on the lake. Still, campers have several decisions to make in picking their ideal site. Paddle over to the Maine side for a chance of spotting moose, but steer toward New Hampshire for sites that are more protected. Island sites are breezy, but closer to motorboat traffic. Hidden coves are quiet, but a favorite haunt of bugs. Whatever your preference, you'll be happier away from the southern base and north of Tidswell Point.

Wherever you establish camp, sooner or later you'll be drawn to the northwest corner of the lake by the chance to spot an eagle. Tapered peaks, bread-loaf summits, and small, pimpled hills form a gentle basin that dwindles to a flat horizon in this isolated corner where the Androscoggin and Magalloway rivers wander off in slack-water channels. Sliding through shallow passes between reeds and marshy islands, boaters in this horizontal region eventually spy a tree topped by a round jumble of sticks that served as an unkempt nest. Eagles haven't paired here for the last several years, but bald eagles still live in this marsh in the summer. If you drift quietly into the scrub that lines a tiny island, you might see a great blue heron standing in the shallows, while high in the branches of a dead tree just a few yards away a male eagle patiently scans the sweep of this northern lake.

Whether paddling in the evening on a wind-still lake or relaxing on a fallen log as darkness covers your camp, Lake Umbagog is a place to watch and listen. Groups of loons cruise between islands, diving for fish on occasion or beating their wings in proud displays that lift them out of the water. Kingfishers loop from tree to tree along the lapping shore, and crook-winged osprey soar from nests on high-level flights in search of another fish. Even after you retire for the evening, the sounds of nature may not end on this bold wilderness lake. Paddlers who love the cries of loons echoing in the dead of night, may not be ready for a full-throated call from the cove next to their tent, and the splashing footsteps of a long-legged moose will be loud enough to give you a start in the silence of a misty dawn.

The practical guide

Access: From the junction of U.S. Highway 2 and New Hampshire Highway 16 in Gorham, follow Highway 16 north 35 miles through the city of Berlin and along the Androscoggin River to the small village of Errol. Turn right onto New Hampshire Highway 26 in the center of the village, and continue straight where Highway 16 bears left at the edge of town. The Umbagog Lake Family Campground is 7.5 miles further east on Highway 26 just 0.3 mile beyond a state-owned boat ramp at the south end of Lake Umbagog.

The shallows of Lake Umbagog near the outlet of the Androscoggin River

The headquarters of the Lake Umbagog National Wildlife Refuge are 5.6 miles north of Errol on New Hampshire Highway 16.

Accommodations and reservations: Reservations are needed to assure a wilderness campsite on any summer weekend. Reservations are also advised to obtain choice

New Hampshire

sites on weekdays throughout the summer. Contact Umbagog Lake Campground at the address below for reservations as well as current rates for campsites, canoe rentals, and boat-transport services.

Maps: A map that locates wilderness campsites is available from Umbagog Lake Campground. See also USGS Umbagog Lake North and Umbagog Lake South quads.

For further information: Umbagog Lake Campground, P.O. Box 181, Errol, NH 03579, Tel. (603) 482-7795; U.S. Fish and Wildlife Service, Lake Umbagog National Wildlife Refuge, P.O. Box 280, Errol, NH 03579, Tel. (603) 482-3415.

New Hampshire

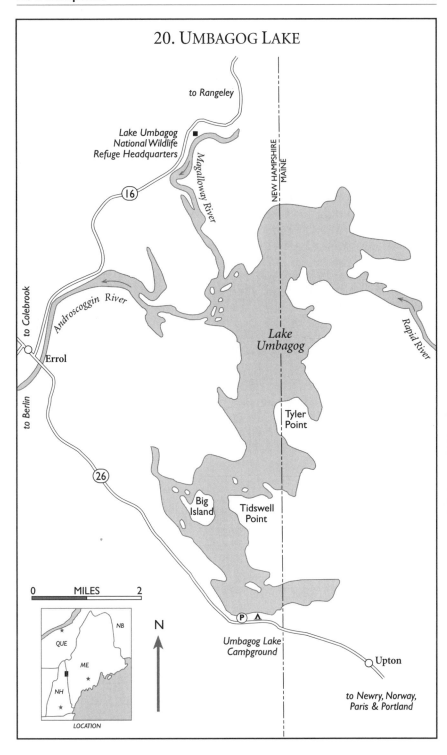

20. UMBAGOG LAKE

to Rangeley

Lake Umbagog
National Wildlife
Refuge Headquarters

Magalloway River

NEW HAMPSHIRE
MAINE

16

Androscoggin River

to Colebrook

Errol

to Berlin

Lake
Umbagog

Rapid River

Tyler
Point

26

Big
Island

Tidswell
Point

0   MILES   2

N

QUE

NB

ME

NH

LOCATION

P ⛺

Umbagog Lake
Campground

Upton

to Newry, Norway,
Paris & Portland

21. The Hut at Zealand Falls

Zealand Notch, White Mountains, New Hampshire

Zealand at a glance

Destination: A streamside hut overlooking Zealand Notch
Location: South of Twin Mountain, between Crawford Notch and Franconia
  Notch in White Mountain National Forest
Access: Gravel road to the summer trailhead, hiking trail to the hut; In
  winter, road and trail are skied from a paved highway
Difficulty: Moderate (almost Easy in summer and fall)
Accommodations: Shared bunkrooms in a mountain hut
Duration: Two or three days
Featured attractions: Zealand Falls, Thoreau Falls, Whitewall Mountain,
  and Zealand Notch

One hundred years ago, steam engines rumbled above Whitewall Brook,
logging trains carried away the remnants of a ravaged forest, and scorch-
ing fires seared what was left in a desolate, plundered landscape. Bat-
tered and misused, a White Mountain "wilderness" came into public hands.
A sordid history of environmental abuse, but visitors to this national forest discover a pleasant surprise. Today, Zealand Notch stands not as a
sobering sight, but rather as a heartening testament to the power of nature's
healing. A practiced eye can still sense a strange mix of vegetation, an odd
precision in the contours of the trails, or the telltale effect of flames on
jumbled rock, but Zealand Notch also contains exquisite New England
scenery and a backpacker's lodge that welcomes outdoor enthusiasts at
any time of year.

Iron tracks and wooden timbers have long since been removed, but
the gentle inclines of railroad beds now serve as four-season pathways
that open this mountain pass to hikers and skiers of average ability. Traversing a former logging grade at the northern entrance to the Pemigewasset
Wilderness, Zealand Road departs the busy corridor of U.S. Highway 302
intent on a scenic rendezvous with a trail that leads to Zealand Notch and
the hut at Zealand Falls. Popular campgrounds flank this forest road that
eases 3.4 miles uphill along the Zealand River, passing fishing holes and
trails to nearby peaks, before dead-ending at a parking area that marks
the Zealand trailhead.

Zealand Road is closed to motor vehicles in winter, and skiers are
required to park their cars back on Highway 302. With a resulting distance
of over six miles from automobile to hut, the self-propelled jaunt over road
and trail is an adventure in itself, especially challenging when the waxing
thermometer at the Zealand Hut tops out at 15 below. Cross-country ski
trails swing through the campgrounds parallel to Zealand Road, but most
winter visitors seem perfectly content to stride and glide to the summer

trailhead on this unplowed forest road that rises at a steady pace.

More than a gentle 2.5-mile access route that ends near a hillside hut, the Zealand Trail affords a mellow walk that meets the Zealand River and traces its many guises to its source near Zealand Pond. Boulder-choked stream, buzzing marsh, placid brook, beaver swamp, and quiet mountain pool entertain on this loitering hike as the chatter of birds in alders and moose tracks in shallow mud promise glimpses of wildlife. Glorious in early fall when blazing crimson colors the maples in the beaver swamps, this family route converts to more subtle beauty in the coldest months, when birch bark and new-fallen snow create studies in winter white.

The Zealand Trail ends at a junction near a corner of Zealand Pond, where the Twinway Trail jogs west to the Zealand Falls Hut, and the Ethan Pond Trail continues south on old railroad grades through spectacular Zealand Notch. Before exploring further, turn right on the Twinway Trail and scramble 0.2 mile to the hillside hut to drop your overnight gear. After crossing a tiny outlet, winter guests stow skis and poles at a platform overlooking a pond, while summer hikers find scenic rewards on brief off-trail excursions to the base of Zealand Falls. Detours concluded, the short, steep, rocky path that scampers up to the hut is actually easier to climb when packed with winter snow.

Beautifully located beside the stream that feeds Zealand Falls, the porch of the Zealand hut surveys the gleaming jumble of Whitewall Mountain on the eastern flank of Zealand Notch and the dark profiles of distant peaks that rise deep in the Pemigewasset Wilderness. Warm-weather hikers have terrific reason to admire additional views. Bathing suits and picnics are the order of the day, as hikers lounge on smooth rocks in the middle of the summer stream with gentle vistas over the top of Zealand Falls to ponds and mountains that separate this valley from popular Crawford Notch.

The Ethan Pond Trail, summer hiking through Zealand Notch

Inside the cabin, visitors find all the essentials that are standard in Appalachian Mountain Club huts: space for 36 guests in two coed bunkrooms, indoor toilets, cold running water, a gaslit dining/sitting room, and a fully-equipped kitchen complete the year-round basics. From late May to mid-October, an energetic crew serves bountiful meals, oversees the hut, and cheerfully demonstrates the proper technique for folding the heavy blankets that lie on every bunk. Still, even in summer, most overnight guests elect to bring sleeping bags, along with snacks, towels, flashlights, and all the personal items they need for a low-key, laid-back, overnight backcountry trip.

Winter guests have to adjust to different rules. From October to May, the Zealand hut operates on a caretaker-only basis. Cooking food they've brought from home, washing dishes, and leaving the kitchen clean, guests are on their own. The shorthanded crew is largely restricted to collecting overnight fees and vigorously enforcing an unwritten code of Spartan wood-stove rules. When fire wood has to be carried all the way from Zealand Pond, heat is a luxury item. Be ready for an afternoon chill and a thick coating of hoary frost on the inside of bunkroom walls when you wake on a winter morning.

The year-round hut at Zealand Falls

Whether on an overnight visit, a weekend retreat, or a relaxed extended stay, guests at Zealand Falls share a wealth of natural attractions. Without venturing more than 1.5 miles from the door of the hillside hut, hikers can dash up the Twinway to breathtaking mountain views, amble about on wetland walks in the environs of Zealand Pond, or refresh tired feet in the icy flow of plunging Whitewall Brook. Eventually though, the alluring view from the front porch proves far too hard to resist, and visitors set off for prolonged treks in beautiful Zealand Notch. After dropping down to the trail junction by peaceful Zealand Pond, guests head south on the Ethan Pond Trail, which departs through evergreen woods as emerging views of Zealand Ridge flicker on the right. Steep, shallow gullies slash across this easygoing trail where long-lost railroad trestles once spanned the pathway's gaps. Barely noticed by summer hikers, these short interruptions give intermediate skiers fits as skis come off to walk these random segments over the course of the next mile. Jumbled boulders and opening sky announce arrival in Zealand Notch, where a long traverse tracks the length of a narrow terrace carved into the side of Whitewall Mountain. Above and below, giant shards of gleaming rock cling to the mountainside, verdant forests blanket a ridge beyond unseen Whitewall Brook, and views of mountaintops seem to extrude from the ends of the narrow notch.

New Hampshire

Though enthralled with the vista from the scenic platform clinging to the side of the notch, you should save time to travel down the line to other premier sites. Less than a mile from the talus slopes in the middle of the mountain pass, the turbulent waters of the North Fork rush over a bed of granite to the lip of Thoreau Falls. Sluicing pools, potholes, and undercut banks of rock leave space for summer picnics on slabs of polished stone as the stream plunges over the brink in a fan of roiling white.

Hikers with plenty of time on their hands have a range of other options that are readily reached on day-trips from the comfort of the Zealand hut. Among the easy walking paths that penetrate the Pemigewasset Wilderness, try cruising to Shoal Pond with lots of berries and moose, or walk along the Appalachian Trail to tiny Ethan Pond, where a lean-to shelter offers memorable views of Mount Willey's striking cliffs.

The practical guide

Access: Zealand Road turns south off U.S. Highway 302 2.1 miles east of the junction of U.S. Highways 3 and 302 in Twin Mountain. Follow Zealand Road past Zealand Campground 3.4 miles to parking at the Zealand trailhead. In winter, when Zealand Road is closed, parking is provided on the north side of U.S. Highway 302 just east of Zealand Road.

Accommodations and reservations: Huts are popular destinations and require advanced reservations. Summer is active, and weekends fill up quickly throughout the year. During the full service (May to October) season, the Zealand Falls Hut serves family-style breakfasts and dinners, and hot drinks and trail snacks are available throughout the day. Bunks have a mattress and wool blanket. Sheets, towels and pillow cases are not provided. Most people bring a sleeping bag. For reservations call the Appalachian Mountain Club at (603) 466-2727 or write the AMC at the address below.

Maps: USGS South Twin Mountain and Crawford Notch quads; also the Appalachian Mountain Club "Franconia" map. Handout trail maps and hike descriptions are also available from the Forest Service Ranger Station listed below.

For further information: Ammonoosuc Ranger Station, Box 239, Bethlehem, NH 03574, Tel. (603) 869-2626; Appalachian Mountain Club, Pinkham Notch Visitor Center, Box 298, Gorham, NH 03581.

New Hampshire

21. THE HUT AT ZEALAND FALLS

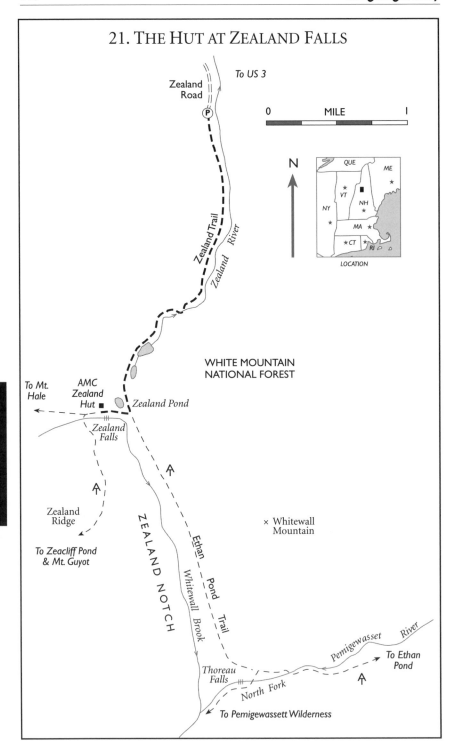

Rhode Island

22. Old Harbor
Block Island, Rhode Island

Block Island at a glance

Destination: Victorian inn or bed and breakfast near Block Island's eastern shore

Location: Between Block Island Sound and the Atlantic Ocean, about 20 miles southwest of Newport, Rhode Island

Access: Auto and passenger ferry service to the island; hike, bike, or drive to the various trailheads

Difficulty: Easy

Accommodations: Comfortable to casually elegant

Duration: Day-trip, overnight, or as long as your schedule allows

Featured attractions: Greenway trails from freshwater marshes to towering bluffs on the ocean shore

Ever wonder what the earth would look like if conservationists ruled the world? One appealing version of the consequences lies just a short ride away on the Block Island Ferry. Designated by The Nature Conservancy as one of twelve "Last Great Places" in the Western Hemisphere, this 6400-acre island twelve miles off the coast thrives as an inspiring model of people and nature working in harmony. Thanks to the timely efforts of conservation organizations, state agencies, and a local community committed to preservation, glowing descriptions of Block Island will forever be more than just public-relations hype. Wander half a mile from the ferry landing in the center of Old Harbor, and neat stone walls, checkerboard pastures, and sweeping ocean vistas instill a palpable sense of coming home to a modern rendition of a bygone era.

Charles Darwin may have been the first to popularize the notion that islands are special places. Though Block Island is no Galapagos, geographic isolation, a unique ecology, and the benign fortunes of history also assure its status as one of the world's extraordinary island environments. More than 40 rare or endangered species and natural communities as diverse as freshwater marshes, kettle-hole ponds, grass-covered dunes, eroding bluffs, scrub-coated hills, morainal grasslands, and rumbling beaches of stone offer curious walkers dense environs for delightful

117

exploration. Strategically located on the Atlantic Flyway, Block Island also comprises a paradise for birders. Sea gulls, shorebirds, and migratory waterfowl are especially prevalent near the beachside dunes of the National Wildlife Refuge at Sandy Point. Raptors that hover above freshwater marshes, swans that cruise about Sachem Pond, and songbirds that winter in upland scrub also delight visitors on this compact island that is now more than 25% preserved as permanent open space.

Of course, human history has also left a mark on Block Island. Developed in an era when steamships carried visitors from east-coast cities directly to the Old Harbor dock, immense hotels line the waterfront in the grand style of that golden age when families flocked to these breezy shores to linger much of the summer. Spruced up and revitalized, Victorian hotels, picturesque inns, and comfortable bed-and-breakfast homes dot the hillsides that surround the harbor, as convenient to ship-born passengers as they were before invention of the horseless carriage. Even today, a large measure of Block Island's character derives from the fact that motor vehicles are just an indulgent option. A wealth of restaurants and accommodations congregate within a five-minute walk of the ferry landing, where burgeoning bicycle and (if you really must) moped rental agencies cater to swarms of car-less tourists. About seven miles long and three-and-a-half miles wide, Block Island is covered with winding lanes that allow bikers and hikers ample chance to explore its nooks and crannies. If you're the least bit comfortable travelling light, rent a bike and leave your mini-van back at Point Judith.

The nucleus of the 25 miles of well-maintained trails that lace Block Island's unique environment is the Greenway network, centered in the southern lobe of this roughly triangular island. From the inland heights of Beacon Hill to the pastoral vistas of Cooneymus Road, granite "Greenway" posts and turnstile gates mark numerous points of access that are linked to an overall plan. Secure a map from The Nature Conservancy's local office, and take your pick of a rich variety of short to mid-length trails that explore an astounding array of habitats.

A moderate walk that features a superb cross section of the island's natural communities begins at the Fresh Pond entrance to the Greenway on Center Road. Scattered homes of weathered gray accent a landscape of rolling fields, ocean views, and broad fresh-air sky, as a section of post-and-rail fence interrupts a low stone wall and guides walkers onto a path at the

Fresh Pond entrance to the greenway at Center Road

edge of a grassy meadow. Descending easily below the limbs of encroaching apple trees, the trampled path crosses a plank bridge at the northwest tip of Fresh Pond, one of the largest of the myriad kettle holes and freshwater pools that pepper this glacier-formed island. Crows and gulls squabble overhead as the trail loops through changing vegetation from meadow to marsh to an upland knoll that boasts a distant outlook across the protected pond.

Beyond the knoll, bear right on a broad swath of green that angles away from the water into the throat of a hilly cleft. Deer tracks lead walkers through a coppice of trees and shrubs aflutter with birds feasting on abundant berries. The path rapidly climbs to a spreading maple near the top of a moderate ridge, where a helpful sign points right, toward Rodman's Hollow. Continue uphill for fifty yards and step through a stone wall. A cleared path now wends its way down through a tangled jungle, deposits hikers at the edge of a narrow dirt road, and resumes by angling off the road about 70 yards ahead on the right. Slicing through dense thickets of scrub, hikers gain a startling sense of seclusion on this downhill amble as visions of human habitations disappear behind the crest of the encircling ridge. In late autumn, a palette of dull orange and muted red enlivens a backdrop of green and brown at the bottom of Rodman's Hollow, a glacial outwash basin that dips below the level of the unseen sea. Songbirds skittering through groves of shadbush impart a timeless solitude to this soothing pocket of nature, where hikers are interrupted only by a wheezy siren that marks the coming of noon for boats that bob in the harbor.

Turn left at a T on the floor of Rodman's Hollow and gradually climb to the opposite rim, where park benches on an overlook knoll end a short detour with views of scrub and sea. The cleared swath of the footpath soon concludes at another turnstile on the edge of Black Rock Road, a pockmarked 4WD track best reserved for hikers and bikers. To the right, the dirt lane leads about one mile north to a Greenway exit on Cooneymus Road, but a dead-end excursion 0.4 mile to the left offers a final variation on exciting island terrain. For a can't-miss conclusion to your hike, turn south and trace the ragged remains of Black Rock Road down a face of corroded cliffs to an angry surf that breaks on a stony beach, or bear right instead at the end of the road onto a path of sand that edges a meadow at the very brink of a seaside cliff. High or low, either course leads to consuming views of ocean waves surging near Black Rock Point, where boulders awash below the sea wait for careless mariners.

Boaters and beach-lovers swell the population of Block Island from late June through mid September, when the Atlantic surf cools bathers on Crescent Beach, and Great Salt Pond comes alive with visiting yachts. Hikers and bikers can certainly coexist with the summer swarm, but a variety of trails and a moderate marine climate make Block Island a natu-

Rhode Island

ral choice for off-season New England hiking. Shadbush blooms in early May or bird migrations throughout the fall are perfect times for relaxed rambles by naturalists. A few inns and eateries even stay open throughout the winter, catering to wanderers who love salt spray, crisp clear air, and paths they can stroll alone. In addition to the Fresh Pond Greenway route, a number of Block Island trails make for memorable walking during any month of the year. Whatever the weather or season, try to find time for as many of the following excursions as you can.

Contemplative in any season, the enchanting Clay Head Nature Trail offers a marvelous half-day option exploring the distinctive coastal environment at the northern tip of Block Island. Travel north from Old Harbor, passing between the Atlantic Ocean and Great Salt Pond on the narrow neck of dunes that holds the island together. A little past Mansion Beach, about 3.5 miles from town, turn right off Corn Neck Road at another granite Greenway post at the end of a narrow dirt road. About 0.5 mile east, you'll find parking and an information kiosk near the trailhead. The oceanward journey continues on foot through a tangle of vegetation, nipping the edge of Clay Head Swamp, with classic wetland views and good prospects for wildlife spotting. Sounds of surf soon signal a change of pace as a spur path leads directly to a rocky beach and the sandy track of the main trail curls to the crest of a seaside bluff. More than a mile of northward strolling waits on top of these breezy cliffs where bayberry and beach rose crowd the path yet still allow views of cormorants perching on rocks below. For extended meanders and a chance to get really lost, turn left onto one of the many paths that penetrate the Maze, a labyrinth of connected trails where freshwater pools, brush-covered fields, and the shade of protective pines add spice to the seaside heights. The Clay Head Trail ends across Corn Neck Road from Sachem Pond, a short walk from a parking area at Settlers Rock and within view of windswept North Light near the very tip of the island.

Set in the dunes on a curve of beach at the head of Sandy Point, North Light oversees the turbulent passage where the clashing currents of Block Island Sound meet the Atlantic Ocean. A magnet for beachcombers who walk about 0.5 mile from the road, this massive granite house topped by a gleaming beacon lies within the Block Island National Wildlife Refuge and includes an interpretive center. The dunes that surround the light are important nesting areas closed to the curious public, but avid birders can still find abundant subjects along miles of pebbly beach.

At the opposite end of the island, the shortest walk on this seaborne refuge remains the most inspiring. Step for step, Southeast Light and the Mohegan Bluffs grant the richest rewards of any Block Island hike. The epitome of ocean cliffs and crashing surf, it's a must stop throughout the year for day-trippers and residents alike. The brick tower of Southeast

*Southeast Light atop
the Mohegan Bluffs*

Light is open for tours during most of the summer season, but visitors have fun just circling this huge Victorian structure and looking back from the brink of the crumbling cliffs where it stood until 1994. A few paces away on West Beach Road, bike racks and a parking turnout mark the Payne Overlook, with a perfect panorama back at the red-brick light surrounded by wind, waves, and the eroded Mohegan cliffs. Regrettably, most visitors stop at the top of the wooden stairs that descend through a gap in the bluffs. The view from the top is sublime, but a walk on the beach works a transformation. Down below, sun, sand, and salty spray crashing on toppled rocks meld with a curious chatter of stones as the tide churns in and out. It's the perfect spot to stroll by the sea and gain insights on the power of nature, the fate of the cliffs above the strand, and the future of Block Island.

The practical guide

Access: Year-round car and passenger ferry service between Block Island and Point Judith, Rhode Island, is provided by Interstate Navigation (401) 783-4613. To reach Point Judith from the south, follow U.S. Highway 1 east from Westerly, Rhode Island, to the junction with Rhode Island Highway 108 near Narragansett. From the north, take Rhode Island highway 4 south from exit 9 on Interstate 95. Highway 4 merges with U.S. Highway 1 a few miles north of the 108 junction. The ferry landing is actually located in Galilee. Follow 108 south 3.0 miles, turn right at the Block Island Boat sign, and then left at the final **T**. Schedules vary with day and season, but car reservations are always a must. The same company or an affiliate also operates seasonal ferry services from Newport, Providence, and New London.

Passenger-only ferry service is also available seasonally from Montauk, New York. Call Viking Lines (516) 668-5700 or Jigger III (516) 668-2214 for New York information.

Regularly scheduled air service to and from Westerly, Rhode Island, is provided by New England Air Lines (800) 243-2460. Action Airlines provides service from LaGuardia airport in New York (800) 243-8623. Charter service is available from Resort Air (401) 466-200 or Block Island Airlines (800) 411-3592.

Accommodations and reservations: From comfortable to downright sybaritic, lodging is abundant on Block Island, although many smaller inns and most large Victorian hotels are closed in the off season. Old Harbor definitely does NOT roll up the sidewalks on summer nights. "Green" visitors may be just as happy to walk, bike, or drive a block or two away from the waterfront and leave the late-night revelry to others. I enjoyed the Sheffield House — (401) 466-5067 — a year-round bed and breakfast with a relaxed blend of comfort and informality, but the Blue Dory (800) 992-7290, Gothic (800) 944-8991, Rose Farm Inn (401) 466-2034, Hotel Manisses (401) 466-2421 or almost any other establishment on High or Spring Street will ably serve a variety of visitor tastes.

Maps: For one dollar and an SASE, The Nature Conservancy (P.O. Box 1287, Block Island, Rhode Island, 02807, Tel. (401) 466-2129) supplies a map and brief descriptions of Block Island Walking Trails.

For further information: The Nature Conservancy information center (mailing address above) at New Harbor on Block Island also offers Nature Walks and Children's programs during the summer and early fall. For a listing of accommodations and general Block Island information contact the Block Island Chamber of Commerce, Drawer D, Block Island, Rhode Island 02807, Tel. (800) 383-BIRI.

22. BLOCK ISLAND

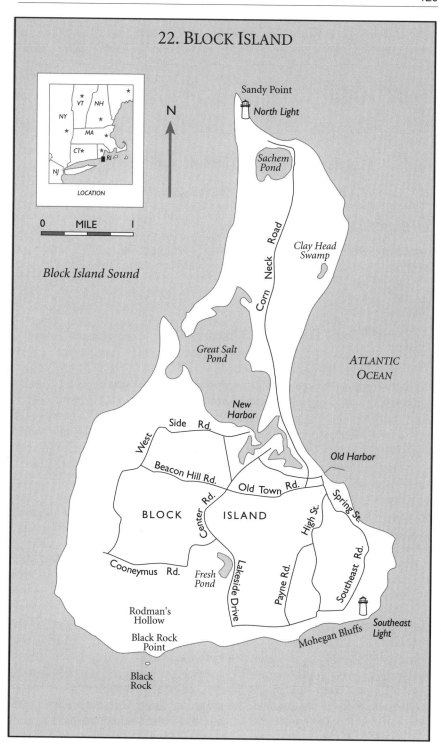

Sandy Point

North Light

N

VT
NH
NY
MA
CT★
RI
NJ

LOCATION

0   MILE   1

Sachem
Pond

Block Island Sound

Corn Neck Road

*Clay Head
Swamp*

*Great Salt
Pond*

ATLANTIC
OCEAN

New
Harbor

Side   Rd.

West

Old Harbor

Beacon Hill Rd.

Old Town   Rd.

Spring St.

BLOCK   ISLAND

Center Rd.

High St.

Cooneymus   Rd.

*Fresh
Pond*

Lakeside Drive

Payne Rd.

Southeast Rd.

Rodman's
Hollow

Southeast
Light

Black Rock
Point

Mohegan Bluffs

Black
Rock

Vermont

23. The Battenkill River

Arlington and Manchester, Vermont

The Battenkill at a glance

Destination: Riverfront inns on a fabled fly-fishing stream
Location: Southwestern Vermont, between Manchester village and the New York border
Access: Paved highways and gravel roads
Difficulty: Easy
Accommodations: From comfortable to elegant
Duration: Weekend or extended stay
Featured attractions: Native brown and brook trout in a tranquil intervale

The Battenkill isn't a secret. Entire books and scads of articles have been written about this river. It's not wild. It's not remote. You'll never fish it alone, but over the course of generations this fabled stream has become a symbol of fly fishing in New England. If you're even slightly familiar with Muddlers and Quill Gordons, the Battenkill can't be avoided. Flowing through a pastoral valley in southwestern Vermont, this legendary river's ripples and pools provide a perfect habitat for wily native trout and a very formidable test of anyone's fishing skills. Close by its brushy shores, anglers are also able to find unrivalled comfort in a collection of historic lodgings restored with fishing in mind. Step out the door of a streamside inn and cast a fly from shore. Take a midday break in an upscale shop, return to fish till dark, and still have time to enjoy a gourmet meal. For the combination of first-class challenge and off-stream indulgence, the Battenkill is the best river in the East.

Before going further, we need to get something straight. This is not some wild western river teeming with lunker trout that are eager to jump in your creel. The Battenkill hasn't been stocked for more than twenty years. Anglers used to stalking hatchery fish and expecting to land their limit will find disappointment on this testing stream. About 80% brown and 20% brook trout lurk in the Battenkill's pools, but only philosophical anglers will leave with a smile on their face, enjoying the process as much as the catch. If you can't deal with the prospect of being skunked by 16-

to-20 inch fish shrewd enough to grow up in this unspoiled river, you should find another stream.

Collecting the waters of several brooks that drain west from the Green Mountains and east from the Taconic Range, the Battenkill gathers itself in the beautiful Vermont Valley between Dorset and Manchester Center. Meandering south through fields and pastures in a pastoral intervale, the river turns sharply west in the middle of Arlington and dashes through a seam in the mountains to the border of New York. More than 14 miles of this famous stream flow through the state of Vermont, but anglers hoping for the biggest browns should focus their search on the last 10 miles, starting south of Manchester village.

Angling for trout on the Battenkill River

Outfitted with chest waders, a long rod, light floating line, and a good selection of flies, drive south from Manchester Center on Vermont Highway 7A. Anglers themselves might be lured to the Orvis store to enroll in casting classes or to buy last-minute supplies, before passing through wealthy Manchester village and turning left onto River Road for an up-close look at what plenty of money can buy. Leading to the junction of River Road with Richville Road at a bridge that crosses the river, a two-mile drive spans the length of impeccable Hildene Meadows, a riverfront landscape below the mansion where Robert Todd Lincoln lived. Narrow, deep, and swiftly moving through bottomland pastures bounded by mountain heights, this beautiful stretch of river that flows under the bridge affords easy access and a perfect habitat for big, homegrown trout.

Especially on the northern portion of River Road from Richville Bridge to a mile below Sunderland, access to the river is sparse. You'll need to distinguish NO HUNTING, NO TRAPPING signs that allow anglers to get to the river from NO TRESPASSING signs, which should stop you in your tracks. Look for parking turnouts and telltale paths that wind down to the bank, and be ready to work your way upstream once you get to the river. As a general rule, access improves the further you travel south and west. Bridge crossings always provide reliable public access, but guests at local lodgings are entitled to exclusive treats. Anchored at either end by two special inns that understand angler's needs, Hill Farm Road connects River Road to Highway 7A. On the eastern end of this short link that crosses the stream just south of Sunderland, red silos, green meadows and superb valley views mark the Hill Farm Inn, a relaxed, traditional country base for enjoying home-cooked meals and a mile of river frontage. On the opposite bank, just north of Hill Farm Road on Highway 7A, the Victorian Battenkill Inn welcomes guests with high ceilings, fireplaces, exceptional dining, and an easy walk out the back door down to the waiting stream.

Anglers who aren't staying at local inns can still get to both banks of the Battenkill River at a few spots south of Hill Farm Road where 7A and River Road parallel either shore. If all else fails, check the "Wagon Wheel" fishing access on the south side of the Highway 7A bridge just above the River Road/7A junction. Provided by the Vermont Department of Fish and Wildlife, brushed-out breaks in a tangled shore give anglers a chance to try their luck casting from steep banks above a deep, tea-colored stream that courses over a sandy bottom.

Overlooking a highway junction that tracks a bend in the stream, the majestic Arlington Inn announces the most promising stretch of the Battenkill River, near the edge of Arlington village. Within view of the Greek columns that line the front of this stately mansion, Vermont Highway 313 bears west and tracks the Battenkill for 6.6 miles as it ends its run in Vermont. Cross the bridge on Highway 313 to the north side of the river just 0.4 mile from the Arlington Inn and you'll confront an enviable choice. To the left, the Rochester Bridge crosses to another section of River Road that follows the south side of the stream while the state highway shadows the opposite bank until the paths rejoin at a new bridge just 0.6 mile east of the state line.

Slightly wider and less deep but moving swiftly on a stony bottom, these beautiful miles of the Battenkill grant anglers idyllic fishing. Wig-

The Arlington Inn, at the edge of Arlington village

Vermont

wagging from side to side between highway and gravel road, the stream seems undecided on where to grant handiest access as steep banks and wooded flatlands alternate from shore to shore. Most anglers will find it helpful to cruise these river loops, picking a spot that corresponds to their skill or their intuition. Between Rochester Bridge and the New York border, you'll find two additional crossings, at Benedict Bridge in two miles and at Covered Bridge in West Arlington, nearly four miles down the line. Crossings again provide convenient stream access and mark the start of worn paths that wander up and down stream. River geography continues to improve the closer you come to the end of Vermont. Flatter, more open banks and a shallower flow that lends itself to wading cut down on tangled flies. As you match wits with native trout, remember to savor the process and try not to be too upset when a lunker brown is scared away by a clumsy thump on the hull of a passing canoe.

Anglers who would like to spend the night on this end of the river have the unique chance to settle themselves into the former home and studio of the painter Norman Rockwell. Set on a rise above the stream just up the road from a red bridge and a gleaming whitewashed church, the Inn On Covered Bridge Green shares apple orchard and river views by the side of River Road. From a comfortable chair on the back lawn, it's a short hop to fishing holes along the south side of the stream and an easy drive to the Red Mill Fishing Access just 0.4 mile shy of the New York border on Highway 313.

Trout season in the Green Mountain State usually runs from mid-April to late October, but warm days, the first natural hatch, and a drop in water volume make mid-May to late June the heart of spring activities. For fabulous foliage and good fishing when trout stoke up for winter, return to the stream to try your luck in September or October. A short section of the Battenkill River west of Arlington is restricted to artificial lures, but elsewhere in Vermont the river can be fished with spinning lures, flies, or even bait. Known as the "Batten Kill" in New York, this excellent stream stretches over the border into that non-New England state where hopeful anglers are strictly limited to fly fishing only.

The practical guide

Access: US Highway 7 runs north and south in western Vermont. For access to Vermont Highway 7A, depart Highway 7 at exit 3 near Arlington or exit 4 near Manchester Center. Highway 7A, Highway 313 in Arlington, and various sections of River Road in Manchester and Arlington provide access to the Battenkill River.

Accommodations and reservations: The greater Manchester area is loaded with inns, bed and breakfasts, motels, and restaurants that cater to alpine skiers, tourists, and shoppers who flock to Manchester Center. In the shadow of Mount Equinox, the famous Equinox Hotel in Manchester village, (802) 362-4700, is probably the most luxurious, but anglers may prefer one of these smaller establishments, which often provide access to the river. Call ahead for reservations and current rates: The Arlington Inn, P.O. Box 369, Arlington, VT 05250, Tel. (800) 443-9442; The Battenkill Inn, Box 948, Manchester Village, VT 05254, Tel. (800) 362-1628; Hill Farm Inn, RR#2 Box 2015, Arlington, VT 05250, Tel. (800) 882-9918; The Inn On Covered Bridge Green, RD 1, Box 3550, Arlington, VT 05250, Tel. (800) 726-9480.

Maps: USGS Manchester, Sunderland, and Arlington quads

For further information: Vermont Department of Fish and Wildlife, 103 S. Main Street, 10 South, Waterbury, VT 05671-0501, Tel. (802) 241-3700.

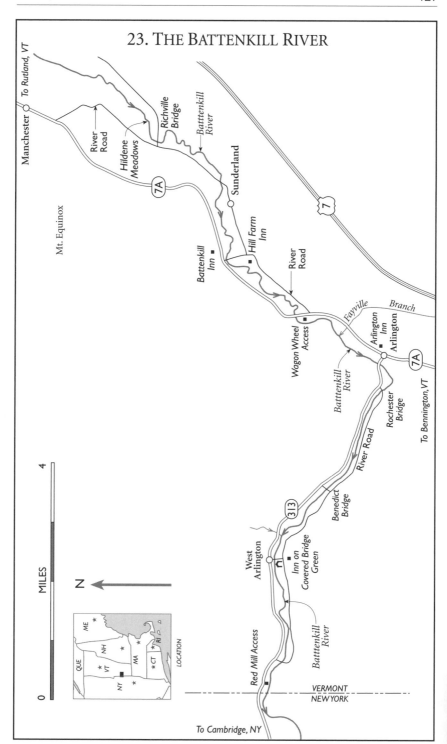

23. THE BATTENKILL RIVER

24. Camel's Hump State Park
Green Mountains, Vermont

Camel's Hump at a glance

Destination: Backpacker's cabins on the forested slopes of Vermont's third-highest peak

Location: About 13 miles west of Montpelier, near Waterbury in central Vermont

Access: Gravel road to the trailhead; hiking trail to huts and summit.

Difficulty: Rough

Accommodations: Very crude cabins

Duration: Overnight

Featured attractions: Magnificent views, scenic ponds, and rare alpine flowers

In spite of Vermont's reputation for scenic alpine splendor, pristine peaks with outstanding views are rare in the Green Mountain State. Climb to the top of most of the highest mountains in Vermont and radio towers, ski lifts, and assorted man-made wonders spoil the backcountry mood. Lower summits tend to be less developed, but overlook limited views. Given the difficult choice between vistas and unspoiled peaks, a National Natural Landmark with infinite panoramas, rare mountain flowers, and no trace of human intrusion is a tempting treat indeed, but the privilege of having the best of both worlds has to be dutifully earned. Rugged trails and the crude comfort of primitive huts are the price you'll pay to experience Camel's Hump, the most appealing summit in the Green Mountain State.

Observed from northern or central Vermont, the sculptured summit of Camel's Hump displays a singular form. Shaped by massive glaciers that tapered its northern flanks and plucked boulders from its southern slopes to create a granite cliff, this pinnacle hovers like a giant fin above an ancient basin that once contained the waters of prehistoric Lake Vermont. Undetected from a distance, a miniature world huddles on this windswept crest, the third-highest peak in Vermont and home to rare varieties of arctic-alpine plants typically found in frigid regions a thousand miles further north. Mosses, lichens, delicate diapensia, deer's hair sedge, and the white blooms of mountain sandwort count among the species that lure naturalists to Camel's Hump, the best preserved of the three Vermont summits that sustain comparable communities of endangered alpine plants.

Various trails converge on this mountain from all points of the compass, but a rare case of good luck makes the least stressful course to this summit also the most scenic route. Beginning near the Couching Lion Farm ranger cabin in Camel's Hump State Park, the Dean, Forestry, and Long Trails conspire to form a loop with fern-filled slopes, alpine ponds, a frontal assault on the face of the peak, and a choice between cabins on the mountain's flanks and campsites near a stream. One long day of hiking will complete this varied tour, but hikers who opt to sleep on these heights can experience a glorious peak when day-tripping crowds don't mass on the summit and muddle the alpine scene.

Passing a spring at the trailhead, the blue-blazed Forestry Trail sidles easily upward on an east-facing slope, rising steadily in the early fall through a forest of cheerful colors — golden ferns, light gray beech, and the muted silvery yellow on the leaves of common birch. Just 1.3 miles from the start, the majority of hikers plod forward on the well-worn Forestry Trail, a direct route straight to the top that misses two miles of the finest hiking in the Green Mountain State. To take the scenic route, bear left instead on the Dean Trail, which dips to cross a creek, spans a stream on a hiker's bridge, and passes a path to a campsite where a streamside glade and tent platforms cater to the self-sufficient. Rapidly increasing its pitch, the Dean Trail soon curls south and climbs to an evergreen world where emerald bogs of moss and sorrel attend an easy ramble to an intimate mountain pond. Tired or not, allow time to pause at this beautiful, silent pool that reflects the summit of Camel's Hump and the cliffs of a rocky ridge between its marshy shores.

Rest stop near Wind Gap with a view of Camel's Hump

Smaller ponds and easy walking draw the Dean Trail to its junction with the Long Trail in Wind Gap, a col between Camel's Hump and Mount Ethan Allen on the Green Mountain crest. To the right, your destination is 1.7 miles north while to the left a shelter known as Montclair Glen Lodge is just 0.2 mile south. Unfortunately, this overnight lodge doesn't match its sumptuous name. A typical Long Trail hut, the "lodge" at Montclair Glen is merely a crude log cabin with wooden bunks, one small table, no heat, and a roof that diverts the rain. Tent platforms and a basic privy complete the accoutrements, except, of course, for intriguing views of Green Mountain peaks that flicker through nearby trees.

North of Wind Gap, hikers find tougher climbing as they push on to the peak. Bouncing from ledge to ledge, the Long Trail executes a remarkably rapid scramble up the end of a mountain ridge as superb views unfold to encompass the ponds you admired below and the majestic scope of the Worcester Range beyond the Mad River Valley. Scurrying up ledges, dipping through woods, and cruising amid glorious views, this northern traverse on the Long Trail edges to a western slope and intimidates hikers with a frontal look at the summit's sheer south wall. Hard to believe you'll be up there, but a tough 0.5 mile climb quickly changes your point of view as the Long Trail exits the woods and meets the Alpine Trail at the base of the summit cone. Apprehension is wasted effort. The last 0.2 mile on the Long Trail is just tough enough to be fun, skipping from boulder to boulder and sneaking past rifts and ribs to conquer the mountaintop.

Surrounded by lawns of endangered flowers and delicate alpine shrubs, volunteer ranger-naturalists from the Green Mountain Club often patrol the summit, reminding hikers to stay on the trail and not trample the vegetation. Tiptoeing from rock to rock on this marvelous compact peak, hikers check the foliage and search for windless resting spots to absorb the fabulous views. In the haze of summer, the worn summits of the Worcester Range and the details of Mount Mansfield's face stand in stark relief beyond the Winooski River, but clear autumn days expand the scene to include a visual feast. Sharp eyes spot the New Hampshire peaks that line Franconia Ridge 60 miles east by a White Mountain notch, while off to the west the flat sheen of Lake Champlain underscores the hulking summits of the High Peaks of New York.

The journey home begins with steps on the Long Trail north, sneaking last glances at Lake Champlain, snaking over a knob, and dropping to a clearing at a junction of trails 0.3 mile from the top. The classic loop bears right at this juncture, making a direct descent on the Forestry Trail, which carries flocks of hikers 3.1 miles back to their cars. For a more secluded alternative, though, and a chance to stay overnight, elude the day-trip crowd by extending your hike a couple of miles through a realm

Green Mountain vistas from the summit of Camel's Hump

of blueberry-covered ledges and perpetual mountain views. Plunging through a mantle of conifers that blankets the northern slopes, a lightly used section of the Long Trail descends just 0.4 mile to another crude cabin beside the path. As primitive as Montclair Glen, the rustic shelter of Gorham Lodge seems a trifle larger, but its real attractions are peace and quiet along with exclusive views of Mount Mansfield lurking beyond a screen of trees at the end of a nearby spur.

After spending the night — or a few quiet moments near the end of a long day hike — leave Gorham Lodge on the Bamforth Ridge Trail for an easy 0.4 mile descent that rolls over open ledges and arrives at a junction with the Alpine Trail amid panoramic outcrop views. (Note: On my last visit in the Fall of 1996, a portion of the Long Trail was rerouted along Bamforth Ridge beginning at Gorham Lodge. Be alert for changes in blazes and signs.) Turn right (south) on the Alpine Trail for an easygoing return that keeps uphill climbing to a minimum and doesn't retrace your steps. Skirting the eastern contours of the mountain well below the summit cone, blueberries, boulders, cobalt sky, and outstanding Worcester Range views dominate this seldom-traveled traverse. Roaming over ribs of barren rock and scampering up naked slabs, the Alpine Trail ascends through a throng of birch and rises to a last panorama in the shadow of the looming peak. It's a fitting farewell to Camel's Hump as the path rolls over a ridge and makes connections with the Forestry Trail 2.5 miles from your car.

The practical guide

Access: From Exit 10 of Interstate 89, follow Vermont Highway 100 South 0.5 mile and turn east at its junction with US Highway 2. Follow the merged highway just over a mile, and where US 2 departs, turn right onto Vermont 100 South. After 0.2 mile turn right on Main Street and continue straight at a sharp curve onto the gravel surface of River Road in about a quarter mile. Follow the river and railroad tracks for 4.9 miles and turn left onto Camel's Hump Road. After 1.1 mile, take the left fork over a bridge and 1.0 mile later continue straight over a second bridge. The narrowing road dead-ends at a parking lot 1.4 miles from the second bridge.

Accommodations and reservations: Not counting clean air and mountain views, Montclair Glen and Gorham lodges furnish little more than bunk space, tables, and a roof over your head. Bring everything you'll need including sleeping bag, foam pad, cookstove and food. Reservations are made by throwing your sleeping bag on a bunk. It's first-come, first-served, but limited use and mountain custom make it rare to be turned away.

Maps: USGS Waterbury and Huntington quads; The Green Mountain Club Guide Book to the Long Trail also contains a useful map of the Camel's Hump trails.

For further information: Department of Forests, Parks and Recreation, District III, 111 West Street, Essex Junction, VT 05452, Tel. (802)879-6565.

Vermont

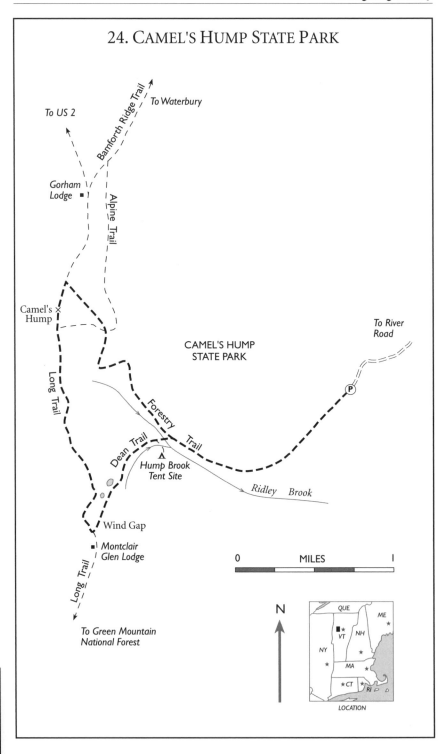

24. CAMEL'S HUMP STATE PARK

To US 2

Bamforth Ridge Trail
To Waterbury

Gorham
Lodge ■

Alpine Trail

Camel's ✕
Hump

CAMEL'S HUMP
STATE PARK

To River
Road

Long Trail

Forestry Trail

P

Dean Trail

Hump Brook
Tent Site

Ridley Brook

Wind Gap

■ Montclair
Glen Lodge

Long Trail

0　　　MILES　　　1

N

To Green Mountain
National Forest

QUE
ME
■★
VT NH
NY
MA
★CT ★ RI

LOCATION

Vermont

25. The Catamount Trail

Green Mountain National Forest, Vermont

The Catamount Trail at a glance

Destination: Inns for cross-country skiers on a backcountry Green Mountain trail

Location: Between Chittenden Reservoir and Brandon Gap, near Rutland in central Vermont

Access: State highways and town roads to inns and trailheads

Difficulty: Moderate

Accommodations: Comfortable to very deluxe

Duration: One or two overnights

Featured attractions: Secluded off-track skiing and mountainous winter views

From the Deerfield River in Massachusetts to US Customs on Canada's border, the Catamount Trail spans the length of Vermont in the shadow of the Green Mountain crest. Designed strictly for winter use, this blue-blazed cross-country route swirls past fields, forests, mountains, and valleys on a varied 280-mile course through the state's most scenic terrain. For much of its length, the Catamount Trail is really an overlay — a blazed route linking logging roads, snowmobile paths, groomed trails, and dedicated rights of way. Conditions vary from ski-center easy to white-knuckle expert descents on this somewhat conceptual route that's subject to gaps here and there and changes from time to time.

On most backcountry sections, advanced intermediates will find themselves up to the task, but you need to know what you're doing. The Catamount Trail Association publishes the Catamount Trail Guidebook, a great tool for prospective skiers, but updates appear in separate newsletters that are more current than the book. Check with the association for up-to-date information, use your wits, and take the Guidebook with a grain of salt.

Cozy inns and cross-country ski resorts are included on the Catamount route. You'll find plenty of chances for great Nordic skiing and old-fashioned country comfort, but backcountry travel from inn to inn is often frustrated by logistics. Romantic treks from door to door are possible on the Catamount Trail (See Chapter 27) but trips are often so long and steep (Bolton to Stowe) or short and commercial (Stowe) that they appeal to few or aren't worth the extra effort. The ten-mile trek from Chittenden Reservoir to Brandon Gap provides a splendid exception — as long as you solve just one logistical glitch.

The fact of the matter is that long midwinter tours through the hills of Vermont aren't meant for solitary skiers. For safety and pleasure you should travel in a group, in which case your problem is solved. Park a car at the junction of Forest Road 406 (FR 406) and Highway 73 near Brandon Gap, drive a second vehicle to the Mountain Top Resort, and cross-country skiers can leave the comfort of a trailside inn, stride through miles of forests, and conclude a day of skiing with a short drive to a choice of exceptional lodgings. Of course, hardy, hard-core, bushwhacking types can break a trail that leads door to door, but more about that later.

A quick look at a topo map makes you believe that direction of travel doesn't matter on this section of trail, but looks can be deceiving. Skiing south to north results in a few moderate climbs and exuberant downhill runs. Starting in the north creates extra work and misses most of the thrill. So begin in the south in Chittenden at the Mountain Top Resort and ski through woods in remote valleys that lead to Brandon Gap just down the road from the Great Cliff near the scenic Green Mountain crest.

Overlooking Chittenden Reservoir, the elegant Mountain Top Inn is a complete four-season resort with 60 miles of cross-country trails, a horse-drawn sleigh, and a hillside lodge with picture-window views of a frozen lake on the floor of a frigid valley. Just a stone's throw from the door of the inn, a ski shop marks the start of your Catamount tour, a handy source for Mountain Top maps, wax, or extra supplies. If you're not an overnight guest you'll pay a daily fee for use of the trails, a fair trade for convenient parking and a downhill start on a well-groomed track. Hop to the opposite side of the access road a little uphill from the shop, ski past a post-and-rail fence, and slide down Hewitt Brook Run across an inclined field with views of Mount Carmel that dominating the distant ridge.

Blue diamonds emblazoned with paw prints distinguish the Cata-

The Lilac Inn, Brandon, Vermont

mount Trail, overlay marks that guide skiers through the maze of named and numbered tracks of Mountain Top's cross-country skiing course. Ski over to Deer Run, which angles north and descends toward the valley floor, bear right on Debonis Cutback, and continue north on Lost Horizon as it loops to junction "56." Bear left on the New Boston Trail, sprint to junction "49," and take your leave of Mountain Top about a mile from where you started, climbing steeply out of bounds and entering Vermont's backcountry in the watershed of Hewitt Brook.

The next nine miles offer skiing at its best, a remote woodland tour that follows a vigorous track just west of the Green Mountain crest. Nestled between the highest peaks and the foothills to the west, this isolated route touches the watersheds of Hewitt, Kiln, and Furnace brooks as it climbs and descends a series of ridges that separate quiet valleys. Out of sight and well protected from the populous Champlain basin, the pitching course darts through a forest of hardwoods, dashes through shallow gaps, and passes under the vigilant gaze of Bloodroot and Goshen mountains. No houses, no barns, no plowed roads intrude on this backcountry route, but skiers are generally pleased to find a touch of domestication.

Snowmobilers and cross-country skiers don't always see eye to eye, but the Vermont Association of Snow Travelers (VAST) supports an extensive network of trails across the entire state that are open to Nordic skiers as well as to snowmobilers. Posted with elaborate maps and signs, many miles of the VAST system are also maintained by a modern grooming machine. Snow conditions change rapidly from day to day, but after you leave the Mountain Top trails, a left turn onto VAST corridor 7 finds a broad, packed swath, wide enough for snowplows and herringbones and perfect for cross-country skiing. Rolling over hill and dale, this VAST track gets limited snowmobile use and is plainly marked with names and numbers corresponding to your destination. If Catamount blazes prove rare and spotty or logging roads intrude, skiers can be confident that trail 73 to Bloodroot Gap leads directly to Highway 73 and the car at their destination.

A packed track doesn't imply easy skiing. Calories burn by the hundreds on frequent, gradual climbs, and adrenalin rush is par for the course on mad downhill runs that twice surprise you with veering right turns at the bottom of steep slopes. A few inches of new snow help, but stiff footwear and steel edges make the tour more pleasant, especially if snow is sparse.

On my last visit, the trail divided 0.25 mile before reaching my destination, with familiar blue paw prints heading off in two directions. Rather than bushwhack an unbroken trail, I stuck with a VAST route that was freshly marked with Catamount blazes and concluded my trek at FR 406 and Highway 73 exactly as I planned.

At the end of a long day, skiers need a dose of comfort. If you'd like to be truly pampered, the elegantly restored Farr mansion houses the Lilac

Striding north on a groomed stretch of the Catamount Trail

Inn about six miles away in Brandon, but two less opulent choices cater
to skiers closer to the end of your tour. Conveniently located on Highway
73 just three miles down the road, the Churchill House offers eight homey
rooms with private baths, Victorian charm, and a sun-filled porch for
relaxing conversations. Less than five miles away on the Goshen/Ripton
Road (FR 32), Blueberry Hill blends a traditional inn with modern accommodations, featuring sauna, rooms with lofts for families, and a delight-
fully leafy sun-room that serves as a corridor. Blueberry Hill and Churchill
House both maintain systems of cross-country trails, which join near Silver Lake, making inn-to-inn outings possible (but not on the Catamount
route) with crystal-clear winter vistas that stretch to the Adirondacks.

For those who dare, the Catamount Trail continues north from Highway 73, but the VAST track you followed comes to a sudden halt. Skiers
are on their own with a blue-blazed, unpacked trail unskied for much of
the winter. The northbound trailhead is about 0.5 mile east (uphill) of the
FR 406 junction. Angling briskly up slope from a sharp bend in the highway, the route meets a powerline that it follows to a gravel road and then
on to FR 224 before joining the Blueberry network and findings its way to
the inn — a tough uphill five-mile trek for dedicated bushwhackers. I was
content to ski "inn-to-inn" with the help of friends and a trusty vehicle.

The practical guide

Access: The Mountain Top Inn in Chittenden can be reached from
US Highway 4 or 7. From US 7, turn east onto Chittenden Road 2 miles

north of the junction of highways 4 and 7 in Rutland. From US 4, turn north onto Meadow Lake Drive in the town of Mendon. Follow signs from the monument in the center of Chittenden to the top of the hill on Mountain Top Road.

The junction of FR 406 and Highway 73 near Brandon Gap at the north end of this Catamount tour is located 1.2 miles west of the point where the Long Trail crosses the highway at the crest of the Green Mountain ridge, or 2 miles east of FR 32. Turnouts on the south side of the highway in the immediate vicinity of FR 406 provide parking for several cars.

To reach Blueberry Hill from FR 406, drive 2 miles west on Highway 73 and turn right onto FR 32 (Capen Hill Road later Goshen/Ripton Road). Follow signs for FR 32 as it turns left and right over Gould Brook and reaches the inn and ski hut in less than 4 miles. Churchill House is directly off Highway 73 one mile west of the junction of FR 32. The Lilac Inn is also on Highway 73 (Park Street) about 6 miles west of FR 406 in the historic town of Brandon.

Accommodations and reservations: Blueberry Hill Inn, Goshen, VT 05733, Tel. (802) 247-6735; Churchill House Inn, RD 3 Box 3265, Brandon, VT 05733, Tel. (802) 247-3300; The Lilac Inn, 53 Park Street, Brandon, VT 05733-1121, Tel. (800) 221-0720; Mountain Top Inn, Box 474, Mountain Top Road, Chittenden, VT 05737 Tel. (800) 445-2100.

Maps: USGS Brandon, Chittenden, and Mount Carmel quads; The VAST map of Vermont Snowmobile Trails can be purchased in many convenience stores in the area, or contact VAST at the address below. Maps of Blueberry Hill, Churchill House, and Mountain Top ski trails are available at the respective inns.

For further information: Catamount Trail Association, P.O. Box 1235, Burlington, VT 05402, Tel. (802) 864-5794; VAST, P.O. Box 839, Montpelier, VT 05602, Tel. (802) 229-0005.

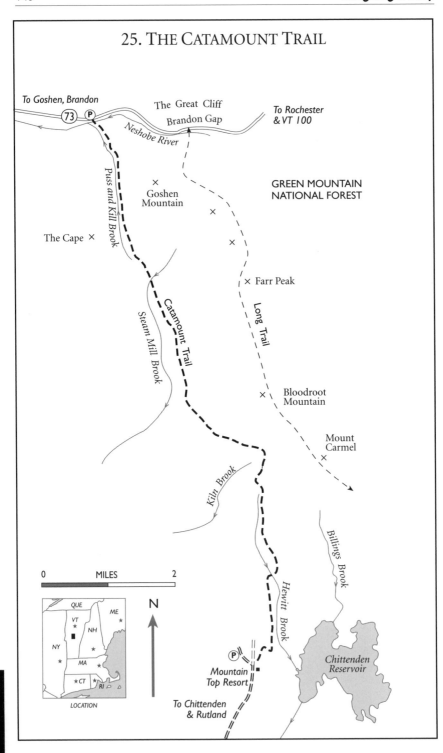

25. THE CATAMOUNT TRAIL

To Goshen, Brandon

73 (P)

The Great Cliff

Brandon Gap

To Rochester & VT 100

Neshobe River

Puss and Kill Brook

× Goshen Mountain

GREEN MOUNTAIN NATIONAL FOREST

The Cape ×

× Farr Peak

Steam Mill Brook

Catamount Trail

Long Trail

× Bloodroot Mountain

Mount Carmel ×

Kiln Brook

Billings Brook

Hewitt Brook

Chittenden Reservoir

0   MILES   2

QUE

ME

VT ★ ★

NH

NY

MA ★

★ CT ★

RI

LOCATION

N

Mountain Top Resort (P)

To Chittenden & Rutland

Vermont

26. The Cold Hollow Mountains
Belvidere, Vermont

Cold Hollow at a glance

Destination: A family-oriented llama trek in the shadow of the Cold Hollow Mountains

Location: About 20 miles north of Stowe in north-central Vermont

Access: Paved highways

Difficulty: Easy

Accommodations: Comfortable country inns

Duration: Full-day or half-day treks

Featured attractions: Covered bridges, quiet woods, four-footed companions, and a catered gourmet lunch

Sooner or later even intrepid outdoor enthusiasts long for a change of pace. A relaxing walk in the woods perhaps, at an easygoing gait, with pleasing views, a cooling stream, and no burden on your back. To make the day complete, imagine someone serving lunch, and maybe answering the questions you have about the forest and mother nature. Aided by gentle llamas, a growing number of experienced guides actually help clients indulge these dreams of leisure with half-day and day-long treks through varied New England terrain.

Plush resorts, small-town inns, and stunning mountain scenes qualify the environs of Stowe, Vermont, as a hot spot for llama trekking. Not that the profile of Mount Mansfield resembles their native Andes, but llamas are content in these northern mountains to tote panniers through meadows and forests with customary aplomb. In several towns in the region, llama ranchers guide families on mellow walks over ski trails, abandoned roads, and forgotten country lanes. Inspired by the promise of a gourmet lunch, I signed on for a half-day trek at the farm of Laurie and Bill Samal in the Cold Hollow Range.

Extending north from the state's highest peak and rugged Smuggler's Notch, the

Easy walking on a country road

Cold Hollow Mountains conclude the Green Mountain chain with a scaled-down, gentler version of Vermont's typical alpine terrain. Only 30 minutes from Stowe's resorts, a portion of these moderate mountains overlooks a branch of the Lamoille River and creates the perfect setting for a soothing llama trek. At Cold Hollow Llamas, in the shadow of Laraway Mountain, the scale of the nearby summit that carries the Long Trail to Canada's border matches the size of the small barn housing Toro and Tumbleweed.

The first order of business upon arrival at a llama ranch is to meet the companion you'll lead, a 280–450 pound relative of a camel, with soft wool and a friendly, but aloof, disposition. Surefooted and agile on feet that end with two padded toes and nails like a parrot's beak, these 3.5–4-foot-tall pack animals don't bite, communicate through body language, and spit only at other llamas. Stay out of the line of fire if a silent quarrel is brewing between llamas and these stoic beasts will dutifully carry up to one third of their body weight in food and gear over almost any terrain even if a child is leading.

Llamas have only two speeds, but nothing you do will convince them to click into running mode. Soon after you're handed the lead line, experienced llamas train you to the pace they prefer, an enforced saunter that suits these treks to people of any age. From grandparents to the youngest toddlers, entire families amble along as equal partners in a llama-governed group. Hyper super-active hiker types can jolly well slow down.

Covered bridges on a rippling stream enhance the mellow mood. Fall into line with your hiking companions on a gravel country road that turns away from the farm and narrows to cross Morgan Bridge, an ancient span that's nearly lost in a flourish of vegetation on a branch of the Lamoille River. With seven years as a llama trekker and a degree in forestry, Laurie Samal keeps the hiking lively as you meander beside the stream. You'll soon identify raspberry leaves that Toro particularly favors, and find yourself chewing yellow birch for the taste of wintergreen.

The rolling contours of foothill ridges pop into distant view as you recross the shallow river on Mill Covered Bridge, a spectacular setting when the brilliant colors of hardwoods blaze on the autumn hills. Summer hikers might pause for a splash in a nearby swimming hole, before jogging left onto an old woods road that angles up the nearest slope. Rising through the cooling shade of the damp New England forest you'll quickly learn that llamas eat almost anything green, while Laurie remains on immediate call to tell you what your friend ingested.

The woods road dwindles to a logging trail and finally a narrow path as you zigzag through the forest, eventually finding a crude gate at the back of a hilltop meadow. The constantly shifting natural scenery occupies your mind on this Cold Hollow excursion while the walk limbers your body without causing undue stress. Still, after a couple of hours of leading a llama, your stomach triggers a strong interest in the food in that animal's pack. By the time you're really hungry, the half-day hike has circled back to a lush meadow where familiar views of Laraway Mountain rise across the valley, and a rim of shade at the edge of the woods provides a comfortable dining spot.

Lunch alfresco in northern Vermont is as delightful as advertised. With the llamas staked and munching clover or simply ruminating, a table unfolds from Toro's pack while place settings and a vase of flowers appear at the edge of the meadow. A sip of ginger lemonade or raspberry tea prepares you for an appetizer chosen from a tempting menu that includes chilled soup (I recommend peach) and marinated fiddleheads. Entrees are even more eclectic, with choices ranging from poached salmon to lamb strips, venison, and seafood antipasto.

Katie and Tumbleweed enjoying lunch below Laraway Mountain

Calories consumed clearly exceed the calories expended on this blissful country hike, especially if you conclude a sumptuous meal with chocolate euphoria bars or gingerbread with pear brandy. Stuffed and a bit lethargic, end your half-day trek with a drowsy stroll back to the barn, with plenty of time to admire baby llamas, say good-bye to your trekking companion, and slowly take your leave.

Full-day hikes burn a few more calories, but enjoy the same cuisine. Substantially longer than the 3–3.5-hour half-day trek, full-day jaunts visit branching streams, pause for lunch near a beaver pond, and explore more vigorous terrain. Whether trekking all day to remote locations or just wandering away from the barn, the concept remains the same: an easygoing country walk at a leisurely llama pace that adds a relaxed dimension to a hike for the entire family.

The practical guide

Access: Cold Hollow Llamas is located on Vermont Highway 109 in the town of Belvidere. From Vermont Highway 100 in the village of Stowe, turn northwest on Vermont Highway 108 (Mountain Road), pass through Smuggler's Notch, and after 17.5 miles turn right following highways 108 and 109 in the town of Jeffersonville. Drive straight through the blinking lights at the junction with Vermont Highway 15, cross a bridge, and turn right onto Highway 109 where Highway 108 forks left. After 7 miles, look for the Post Office as you pass through the town of Waterville. Cold Hollow Llamas is on the left exactly 3.5 miles beyond the Waterville Post Office.

Accommodations and reservations: Date, number of people, menu selections, and duration of treks must all be arranged in advance. A short season and the growing popularity of llama trekking means it's best not to delay making plans. Most farms can comfortably guide as few as one or two or as many as eight or ten people. For specific costs, menu options, and destinations contact the farms listed under "For Further Information" below.

The following resorts, inns, and bed-and-breakfast homes are within a 30-minute drive of Cold Hollow Llamas: The Inn on Trout River, P.O. Box 76, The Main Street, Montgomery Center, VT 05471-0076, Tel. (800) 338-7049; The Jefferson House, P.O. Box 288, Main Street, Jeffersonville, VT 05464, Tel. (800) 252-9630; Mannsview Inn, Box 4319, Route 108 South, Jeffersonville, VT 05464, Tel. (888) 937-MANN; Smuggler's Notch, Vermont, 05464-9599, Tel. (800) 451-8752

Maps: Maps aren't needed for guided hikes, but see USGS Johnson and Cold Hollow Mountains quads for this portion of the Cold Hollow Range.

For further information: Cold Hollow Llamas, RR1 Box 1019, Belvidere, VT 05492, Tel. (802) 644-5846; Applecheek Farm, RD1, Box 6200, Morrisville, VT 05661, Tel. (802) 888-4482; Green Mountain Expeditions, RR 1, Box 51B, Whitingham, VT 05361, Tel. (802) 368-7147; Northeast Kingdom Llama Expeditions, 152 Heath Brook Road, Groton, VT 05046, Tel. (802) 584-3198; Northern Vermont Llama Co., RD 1, Box 544, Waterville, VT 05492, Tel. (802) 644-2257; Stowe Llama Ranch, 2363 West Hill Road, Stowe, VT 05672, Tel. (802) 253-5118.

27. Craftsbury Common

Northeast Kingdom, Vermont

Craftsbury at a glance

Destination: Country inns and lodges linked by backroads and ski trails in Vermont's Northeast Kingdom

Location: North-central Vermont, about midway between Montpelier and the Canadian border

Access: Paved highways and gravel roads directly to inns and trailheads

Difficulty: Easy to Moderate

Accommodations: Cozy lodges and elegant inns

Duration: Weekend or overnight

Featured attractions: Biking or skiing from village to village in rural northern Vermont with lake and mountain views

Craftsbury Common is one of those places you can't get to from here. First, as they say in New England, you've got to travel somewhere else. Stuck in the northern uplands between the Green and the White Mountains, this rural village can't even claim to be on the way to some other popular spot. The peaks in the region are far too low to attract downhill skiers, and over the years short summers, rocky fields, and miles of boreal forest have even discouraged local farming. At times, of course, being remote creates its own reward. For cross-country skiers or mountain bikers trying to escape crowds, Craftsbury Common is downright ideal.

Winter is the height of Craftsbury's season, with two Nordic ski centers astride the Catamount Trail, the backwoods cross-country ski route that runs the length of Vermont. From the Craftsbury Nordic Ski Center to the tracks of Highland Lodge, more than 100 miles of maintained trails wander over the countryside connecting scattered settlements and local inns. But well-groomed trails and warming huts don't account for Craftsbury's charm, and to picture it as a typical ski resort is to totally miss the point. This is no golf-course ski mecca with trails through manicured woods. The special attraction of Craftsbury Common is the overwhelming sense that you're kicking and gliding through a vital slice of genuine rural life.

As you ski from village to village, enough farms still survive that sloping fields dot the landscape with scenes of patchwork pastures, fleeting glimpses of distant summits, and views of narrow lakes. Coast to a country store down in the hollow in Craftsbury Village, or slide past a church at the top of the hill at the edge of a public common. Ski through meadows and apple orchards along a split-rail fence. Weave through a stately sugarbush cloaked in winter white. Pass a sagging barn sheltering a herd of patient cattle, or skim by the porch of a back-road house that sits in a frozen field. Wherever a ski track leads in this corner of the

Northeast Kingdom, you're immersed in everyday life.

The network of trails maintained by the Craftsbury Nordic Ski Center extends north from Craftsbury Village, encompassing both the settlement at Craftsbury Common and the area around the Craftsbury Outdoor Center just east of Big Hosmer Pond. Connected to Craftsbury Village by a solitary track that wobbles south and east, the trails managed by Highland Lodge circle north of Caspian Lake, including a stretch down Long Pond and a gentle climb to distant views from the top of Barr Hill. The combined networks are so extensive that skiers can roam from inn to inn across the entire system, or simply stay put in a single lodge to enjoy restful runs on local loops and trails.

In addition to food and lodging at the cross-country centers at either end of the system, independent inns and bed-and-breakfast homes offer fabulous getaway options. High above the western shore of Little Hosmer Pond, a colonial farm now serves as the Craftsbury Bed and Breakfast on Wylie Hill, just a short hop from the Catamount Trail as it heads out of town and connected to the Craftsbury system by a glide down the Marathon Trail. Both the Craftsbury Inn in Craftsbury Village across from the country store and the Brassknocker Bed and Breakfast in the hamlet of East Craftsbury place guests at the center of the system on the lonely track that rambles over hill and dale and links village to village.

The most pleasing accommodation, though, is the elegant Inn on the Common, a quiet spot by the side of the road that conveys a country feel behind a white picket fence and a cluster of ancient maples. Queen size beds, fireplaces, fine wines, and gourmet entrees like Cherry Planked Salmon and Pepper Crusted Pork Loin with Brandy Demi-Glace cap a special day of skiing. Winter guests can dine at ease knowing calories will come off tomorrow. After a filling breakfast, venture out of the inn and try an easy jaunt on Trail #50 along the Black River, or follow discreet Catamount signs on Trail #4 as it angles off the hill, passes farms in a lake-filled hollow, and climbs to the heart of the Nordic network by way of Duck Pond.

The Inn on the Common, Craftsbury Common

With the coming of Spring, groomed tracks disappear, gaps in fences close, and livestock return to the pastures — a message to Craftsbury visitors that it's time to hit the road. Remember, though, you're in the Northeast Kingdom, and bicycling here is not what you might expect. With few exceptions, roads in the Craftsbury region remain unpaved and lack descriptive names. Town highways are simply referred to by number, and sign posts like TH #28 guide you on your way. Wandering over hills and valleys in a startling profusion, these country roads experience little traffic and create a welcome paradise for bikers of varied skills.

Transformed into a cycling hub, the Craftsbury Nordic Center is an indispensable stop for mountain bikers, where rentals, repairs, friendly advice, and maps are well supplied. The inexperienced find clinics and guided tours, but most people are perfectly happy to go it on their own. Next to the fruit drinks and soda, a selection of wines in the refreshment cooler at the center gives a hint of the mellow tone. For a little variety, you can even walk down to the dock for a dip in the quiet pond or take a beginner's lesson on one of the center's single sculls.

Backroad views from the Ridge Loop in Vermont's Northeast Kingdom

Bicyclists select their routes from an ample array of options. Readymade maps and tour descriptions are yours for the asking at the Craftsbury Outdoor Center. If you're short on time, a seven-mile jaunt circles the nearby pond, and the two-hour "ridge loop" skims through alpine meadows typical of the Northeast Kingdom. Seen from this wide upland plateau, miles of rumpled pastures and dense spruce/fir forests spread below the summits of Camel's Hump, Mount Mansfield, the Cold Hollow Mountains, and the beautiful Worcester Range. For a longer excursion and equally terrific views, try the full-day Greensboro tour, a back-road variation on a classic Vermont ride. This 27-mile extravaganza passes most of the area's inns, circles Caspian Lake, and leads to the door of The Willey's Store, a legendary purveyor of all the practical merchandise that a north-country resident needs.

The practical guide

Access: Craftsbury Common is truly remote. From Montpelier, take U.S. Highway 2 to East Montpelier and then bear left onto Vermont Highway 14 north. Follow Highway 14, 19 miles to the town of Hardwick, jog left (northwest) on Highway 15, and right (north) again on Highway 14 a little west of town. Travel 6.9 miles as Highway 14 skirts west of Hardwick Lake, passes a public fishing access, and soon finds signs for a right turn to Craftsbury and Craftsbury Common. This paved "town highway" is unmarked, but ample signs direct travellers either straight ahead to Craftsbury Village, Craftsbury Common, and the Craftsbury Nordic Ski Center, or to the right for Brassknocker Bed and Breakfast, East Craftsbury, and Highland Lodge.

Accommodations and reservations: Brassknocker Bed and Breakfast, RR 1, Box 89A, Craftsbury, VT 05826, Tel. (802) 586-2814; Craftsbury Bed and Breakfast on Wylie Hill, Wylie Hill, Craftsbury Common, VT 05827, Tel. (802) 586-2206; Craftsbury Inn, Main Street, Craftsbury, VT 05826, Tel. (800) 336-2848; Craftsbury Nordic Ski Center, Box 31, Craftsbury Common, VT 05827, Tel. (800) 729-7751; Highland Lodge, Caspian Lake, Greensboro, VT 05841, Tel. (802) 533-2647; Inn on the Common, Main Street, Craftsbury Common, VT 05827, Tel. (800) 521-2233.

Fees apply for use of the trails maintained by the Craftsbury Nordic Ski Center and Highland Lodge, but passes are recognized by either center and are good on any trail.

No fees are charged for mountain biking.

Maps: Maps of cross-country ski trails are available at the Craftsbury Nordic Ski Center and at Highland Lodge. Mountain biking maps are available at the Craftsbury Outdoor Center.

For further information: Craftsbury Outdoor Center, Post Office Box 31, Craftsbury Common, VT 05827, Tel. (800) 729-7751; The Catamount Trail Association, PO Box 1235, Burlington, VT 05402, Tel. (802) 864-5794.

28. The Northern Frontier

Montgomery Center, Vermont

Montgomery Center at a glance

Destination: A rural-highway bicycle tour in remote northern Vermont
Location: Between Newport and St. Albans, a few miles south of Canada's border
Access: Paved highways
Difficulty: Moderate
Accommodations: Comfortable country inns
Duration: Weekend or overnight
Featured attractions: Covered bridges, country byways, and northern Green Mountain views

Caught between the final miles of Green Mountain peaks and the lowlands of the Champlain basin, this corner of northern Vermont embraces a rolling landscape that was once washed by the waters of prehistoric Lake Vermont. Subdued long ago by glaciers and erosion, the domesticated hills of this agricultural region are perfectly suited to bicycle tours, with moderate slopes, scarce traffic, and paved rural roads. A classic expedition, this 27-mile circuit explores portions of the Trout River and Missisquoi River valleys, grazes the western slopes of the Cold Hollow Mountains, and grants views of major peaks without climbing difficult hills.

Autumn is the prime time to ride this popular loop. Swamp maples burst with color as early as the first of September, and the vivid hues of Vermont hardwoods erupt into full display by the end of the same month. By Columbus Day, peak colors have faded this far north, but the landscape holds other surprises. Black-and-white cattle lounge in pastures beneath sculptured mountaintops, great blue herons rise from the banks of nimbly flowing streams, and wild turkeys have even been known to amble along the roads.

The tour originates in Montgomery Center, a crossroads town in the valley of the Trout River but under the influence of Jay Peak. Close to a hub of alpine skiing, this northern village with a herd of Holsteins living at the edge of town supports an ample share of restaurants and country inns. Standing side-by-side on Main Street and backing up to the scenic stream, The Inn on Trout River and Phineas Swann Bed & Breakfast serve as possible headquarters for your classic country tour. Both offer brass beds, century-old Victorian charm, wood-burning stoves, antiques, and selections of wholesome food.

Even as you arrive in town, you're likely to gain a sense of greater Montgomery as the covered-bridge center of Vermont. No less than seven post-and-beam covered bridges span the brooks and rivers that flow into this compact valley. Most remarkable of all is that each of these lattice-type structures was built by the same two brothers more than 100 years ago. Owners of a nearby sawmill, Savannah and Sheldon Jewett milled the hemlock and designed the bridges that still carry cars and bicycles across the local streams. Before you pedal north, bridge lovers and history buffs should take a quick spin south to Gibou and Hutchins Bridge roads off Highway 118, where two covered bridges stand close to the main road.

Beginning the round trip, Vermont Highway 118 slides easily out of town, skimming pastures and cornfields that line the Trout River. The easy-pedaling byway rolls 2.4 miles north, traversing a narrow valley through a gauntlet of lumpy hills before reaching another junction at the Montgomery village green. To the right, South Richford Road wanders off as your ultimate route of return. Bear left for now on 118 as it edges the grassy common, passes the local historical society, and finds the Black Lantern Inn. Built in 1803 and listed on the National Register of Historic Places, the Black Lantern is another delightful alternative as a base for your northern tour. Beamed ceilings, candlelight dinners, homemade bread, a comfortable parlor, fireplaces, and jacuzzis, make this popular lodging an outstanding choice to refresh and restore bodies that may not be used to pedaling the knobby Vermont hills.

Passing beyond Montgomery, 118 crosses the river and discovers two more covered bridges built by the Jewett brothers. The Longley Bridge, 1.1 mile north of town, and the Hopkins bridge, just 0.4 mile later, are similar lattice-type structures built near the end of the Civil War. Both allow space for rest and appreciation, but only the Longley Bridge remains open to traffic.

Highway 118 weaves back across the Trout River as it approaches East Berkshire and the junction with Highway 105 4.8 miles from the Montgomery village green. Jog left at a **T** after crossing the Missisquoi River and then turn right only 0.1 mile later, staying on 118 as it starts its moderate climb out of the valley. In just under a mile, pedalers reach the top of the first rise near the Berkshire fire station, where distant peaks poke through the far horizon. The skyline expands in all directions in the next two miles, as the road climbs steadily higher through pastures and fields of corn. Rolling over the final crest, the highest summits of the Green Mountains emerge behind your back, and the highway begins a 1.3-mile glide to the Berkshire Elementary School.

Turn right at the sign that points left to the Town Clerk's office in Berkshire Center and you'll be riding on Richford Road. Rising in measured stages for another moderate mile, this paved country highway tops the last long hill of the day before rushing down the opposite side in an undulating descent. Hit the brakes from time to time to absorb marvelous views of the broad Missisquoi Valley and the looming massif of Jay Peak, with its unmistakable tramway station cantilevered off the top.

Vermont

Profile of the Jay Peak massif from the height of Richford Road

Richford Road ends at a T about a mile from Canada's border. To stay in this country, turn right on River Road, cross a one-lane bridge, and enter the town of Richford. As you near the faded center of this old industrial town, you'll find a gazebo in a public park on the banks of the Missisquoi River. Turn right at a blinker, pass silent mills as you cross the river, and ease through the middle of town. At the end of the business district, turn left at another blinker onto Vermont Highway 105 East, but stay on this busy route for only .7 mile. As you edge out of town, turn right onto unsigned South Richford Road, which angles up a hill opposite an obvious oxbow bend in the shallow Missisquoi River.

A steep climb on South Richford Road lasts only 0.4 mile. With eastern views of the Missisquoi Valley and glimpses into Quebec, this quiet road begins a varied but mostly downhill 7.1-mile run. Coasting through aisles in hardwood forests and sweeping by sidehill pastures, the roller-coaster ride discovers a bumpy landscape more typical of Vermont. Rushing to its conclusion, South Richford Road quickly drops to the Fuller Bridge, the last covered bridge in Montgomery, which carries you across Black Falls Brook just a stone's throw from the village green and Highway 118. Flanked by shading maples, it's a colorful end to a north-country tour, especially in the fall.

About 6 miles east of Montgomery Center on unpaved Vermont Highway 58, Hazens Notch State Park is a possible detour for mountain bikers. Except for a Long Trail crossing, there are no facilities in the park, but the gravel road rising into the notch makes a vigorous backcountry ride. In July of 1997, however, torrential rains brought devastating floods to the Trout River Valley. Homes were destroyed, river banks gouged, and Highway 58 closed for the rest of the summer. The inns and covered bridges survived, and cleanup is underway. By the time this book is published, the road should be open again, and the town should be on the mend.

The practical guide

Access: From exit 10 of Interstate 89, follow Vermont Highway 100 North through Stowe. Stay on Highway 100 as it winds through Morrisville and Hyde Park. In Eden, turn left onto Vermont Highway 118 across from the general store. After 6.5 miles, bear right with Highway 118 as it passes through Belvidere Corners and arrive in Montgomery Center 8.1 miles later.

From exit 26 of Interstate 91, Montgomery Center is 23.6 miles west on Vermont Highway 58. Note, however, that portions of Highway 58 near Hazens Notch are closed during the winter.

Accommodations and reservations: The Black Lantern Inn, Route 118, Montgomery Village, VT 05470, Tel. (800) 255-8661; The Inn On Trout River, P.O. Box 76, The Main Street, Montgomery Center, VT 05471-0076, Tel. (800) 338-7049; Phineas Swann Bed & Breakfast, Main Street, Box 43, Montgomery Center, VT 05471, Tel. (802) 326-4306

Maps: USGS Richford, Jay Peak, and Hazens Notch quads; The Vermont Attractions Association also publishes a free Vermont Attractions Map and Guide available at highway rest stops and information centers.

For further information: Vermont Attractions Association, Box 1284, Montpelier, VT 05601, Tel. (802) 229-4581.

The Missisquoi River, Richford, and distant Jay Peak

28. MONTGOMERY CENTER

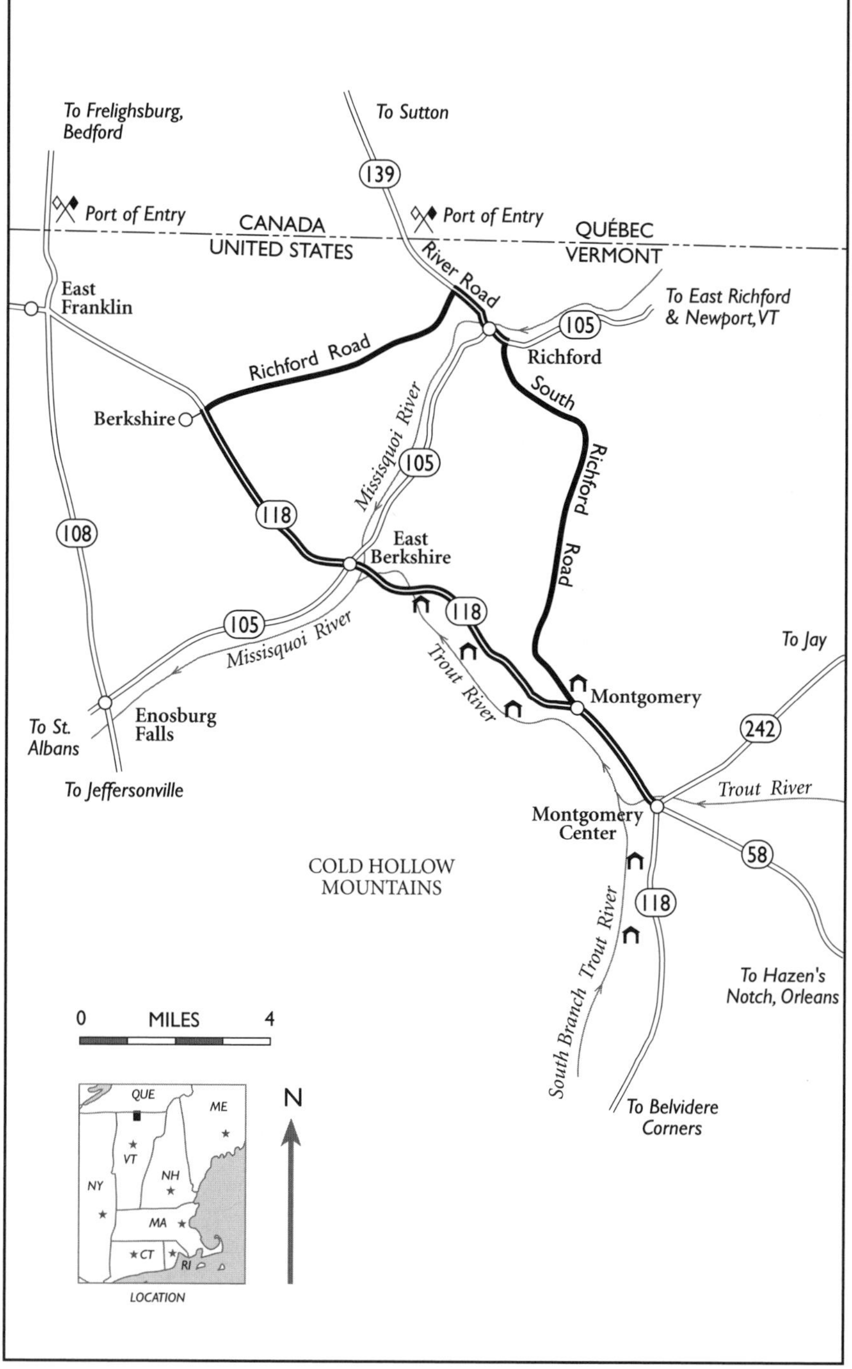

To Frelighsburg,
Bedford

To Sutton

139

Port of Entry

CANADA
UNITED STATES

Port of Entry

QUÉBEC
VERMONT

River Road

East
Franklin

To East Richford
& Newport, VT

105

Richford Road

Richford

Berkshire

Missisquoi River

South

Richford

Road

105

118

East
Berkshire

105

118

To Jay

Missisquoi River

Trout River

Montgomery

242

To St.
Albans

Enosburg
Falls

To Jeffersonville

Trout River

Montgomery
Center

COLD HOLLOW
MOUNTAINS

58

118

South Branch Trout River

To Hazen's
Notch, Orleans

0   MILES   4

To Belvidere
Corners

QUE

ME

N

VT

NH

NY

MA

CT

RI

LOCATION

29. Seyon Recreation Area
Groton State Forest, Vermont

Seyon at a glance

Destination: Seyon Ranch on Noyes Pond
Location: Between US Highways 2 and 302, about fifteen miles east of
    Montpelier, Vermont
Access: Paved and gravel roads suitable for family vehicles
Difficulty: Easy
Accommodations: Rustic
Duration: One to three nights
Featured attractions: Brook trout at Noyes Pond with campgrounds,
    beaches, and multiuse trails throughout Groton State Forest

Rambling, rustic, and rather run down, Seyon Ranch isn't a stop for the
cozy-inn-by-the-lake crowd. Straddling the headwaters of the South Branch
of the Wells River in a corner of Groton State Forest, Seyon Recreation Area
serves a select clientele, that peculiar breed who understands that a little
discomfort isn't too high a price for the chance to catch a trout.

Site of a lumber mill during the heyday of the railroad and timber booms
in the last half of the 19th century, man-made Noyes Pond was converted to
other uses after logging and fires ravaged the local woods. As the State of
Vermont began to acquire the scattered parcels that became Groton State
Forest, conversion of a dam to electric generation and guest-house construction near the eastern shore transformed the onetime sawmill into the Seyon

Canoe landing on Noyes Pond

Trout Ranch, a private brook-
trout preserve. Today, hardwood forests have reclaimed the
surrounding hills, and the Vermont Department of Forests,
Parks and Recreation manages
this backwoods lake as a haven
for devotees who strive to land
squaretail trout with the lure of
fragile flies.

Private vessels aren't welcome on these fly-fishing-only
waters, but a sheltered basin
shielded by pines a few paces
from the lodge offers guests and
day-use visitors a fine selection
of state-owned boats and alu-
minum canoes. A tiny boat
house and several slips arrayed
near the outlet dam provide all

the amenities you'll need, along with commanding views of Spruce Mountain reflecting in the rippled surface that stretches to the west. Small enough to paddle its length in the span of twenty minutes, yet large enough to serve as habitat for roaming moose and loons, Noyes Pond denies its turbulent history with unspoiled woodland scenes. Float its margins casting for trout along a wooded shore or cruise to a marshy inlet at its shallow western rim. Lucky visitors are entertained by a kingfisher's scalloped flight and calmed by verdant upland hills that hide all signs of modern life. A perfect fishing hole.

Regrettably, the guest house at Seyon Ranch is less impressive than the views. Nothing that a good refurbishing wouldn't cure, but painted floors, iron beds, folding chairs, and metal tables create a Spartan look that's a little uninviting. On the other hand, the front-porch chairs are worn to the point of comfort, and the antlered moose head high on the wall lends an air of contemplation. Surveying a broad lawn dotted with tables and grills, the sunlit porch is a natural spot to discuss the latest hatch and exchange expert opinions about which flies might really work.

The innkeeper and his family who live at Seyon Ranch serve three home-cooked meals each day, share a wealth of local knowledge, and generally make sure that the camp delivers comfort where it counts. Hot showers, dry beds, linens, blankets, and towels await guests after a long day on the pond, while a crackling fire and excellent meals do their part to encourage sleep. Any fault with the facilities is quickly overcome by ample portions of good food and friendly, sage advice. You'll be warm and dry and have a full stomach with another day of fishing ahead.

When the sun is high and the fish aren't biting, 25,000-acre Groton State Forest offers plenty of alternate action just a short jaunt up the road. Sprawling across a rumpled landscape a few miles west of the Connecticut Valley, these ragged uplands of forest and bog between the dominant White and Green Mountains are typical of northern Vermont — a favorite spot for "wilderness" camps for nearly 100 years. The comfortable campgrounds and sandy beaches that line Lake Groton's shore retain the old traditions, making Groton State Forest a convenient option for anglers who like to camp and a popular destination for savvy parents looking for family recreation. Reliable access to the center of the forest is provided by Highway 232, which parallels the abandoned bed of the old Montpelier-Wells River Railroad. This

Boat basin at Seyon Ranch

historic line, which once transported logs and passengers to and from the capital of Vermont, now functions as a multiuse link in a year-round network of forest trails. Hike, ski, or snowmobile to the hidden corners of this far-flung forest. For a break from your fishing duties, walk the shore of Kettle Pond, or explore the unspoiled wetlands of impressive Peacham Bog.

The shortest hike in Groton State Forest is by far the most impressive, a can't-miss affair even on those occasions when stubborn trout allow little time to spare. About a mile beyond Kettle Pond toward the northern end of the forest, an auto road branches east off Highway 232 and climbs to a picnic shelter just yards below Owls Head's startling peak. A round-trip walk of only 0.25 mile leads hikers of all generations to the base of a fieldstone tower and outcrop views of forests and ponds that flank this friendly top. Wander about the granite mounds for a series of distant views. Find Osmore Pond and Peacham Pond in the woods rolling north and east, or spot Kettle Pond as it points an arm to the summit of Camel's Hump 30 miles distant on the hazy Green Mountain crest.

The practical guide

Access: Seyon Pond Road intersects US Highway 302, 7 miles east of the intersection of US 302 and Vermont Highway 25. From the Montpelier area simply follow 302 east through Barre and Websterville past the junction with 25 to Seyon Pond Road (the road to Seyon Ranch and Noyes Pond). From the south, depart Interstate 91 at exit 16, follow the Waits River and Highway 25 about 17 miles to US Highway 302, and then turn right on 302 to Seyon Pond Road.

Running north from US 302, gravel Seyon Pond Road is a 3 mile access road that bears right after 1.2 miles and then continues straight, dead-ending at Seyon Ranch.

Seyon Pond Road is also 1 mile west of the junction of US Highway 302 and Vermont 232, the state highway that bisects Groton State Forest and provides access to trails, beaches, campgrounds, and the Owls Head auto road.

Accommodations and reservations: The arrangement of rooms and shared baths at Seyon Ranch results in a preference for families or small groups when making reservations. Individuals can reserve space, if available, not sooner than two weeks prior to arrival. Private and semiprivate sleeping quarters are provided for up to 15 guests. Maximum stay is three nights. During the season (May through October) contact: Seyon Recreation Area, Groton, VT 05046, Tel. (802) 584-3829; November through April contact: Park Regional Manager, Department of Forests, Parks & Recreation, 324 North Main St., Barre, VT 05641, Tel. (802) 479-3241

Maps: USGS Knox Mountain quad; maps of Groton State Forest are available at Seyon Ranch, at nearby campgrounds, or from the address below.

For further information: Agency of Natural Resources, Department of Forests, Parks and Recreation, District V, St. Johnsbury, VT 05819, Tel. (802) 748-8787.

30. Skyline Lodge
Bread Loaf Wilderness, Vermont

Skyline at a glance

Destination: Hillside cabin overlooking a pond in the heart of the Bread Loaf Wilderness.

Location: Green Mountain National Forest, about 11 miles east of Middlebury, Vermont.

Access: Gravel forest road to the trailhead; hiking trail to Skyline Lodge

Difficulty: Moderate

Accommodations: Rustic cabin

Duration: Day hike or short overnight

Featured attractions: Skylight Pond, alpine views, Battell and Bread Loaf mountains.

Mellow walks to mountaintops are few and far between. Add a modern log cabin overlooking a pond just below a mountain crest to lily pads, moose, and alpine views in the heart of a wilderness zone, and your backcountry destination sounds too good to be true. In fact, this straightforward walk to the Green Mountain ridge between Battell and Bread Loaf mountains is well known to local hikers, a convenient day-trip or overnight on a moderate feeder path connected to a long-distance system of trails that spans the length of Vermont.

Completed in 1930 under the guidance of the Green Mountain Club, the Long Trail runs 265 miles from its origins in Massachusetts to a post on Canada's border. More than a primitive route cut through the northern forests, this "footpath in the wilderness" is designed for extended treks along the Green Mountain ridge with an ample array of overnight lodging and feeder trails for rest and resupply. Accommodations vary from simple board huts to lean-tos and rustic shelters, but the peeled-log cabin known as Skyline Lodge grandly exceeds the usual Long Trail standard. Overlooking Skylight Pond and a sea of summits east of the nearby ridge, this secluded hut offers a double-decker sleeping loft, a picturesque porch for sharing views, and reliable quarters on an evergreen slope near the core of the Bread Loaf Wilderness.

Blanketing more than 21,000 acres of mountainous ridges and alpine peaks, Bread Loaf is the largest wilderness in Green Mountain National Forest, an untrammeled zone where human "improvements" won't disrupt the primitive feel. Itinerant clangs and buzzes don't echo in this quiet land, where chain saws, mountain bikes, and motorized and mechanical equipment are forever strictly banned. Located on a spur just 0.1 mile east of a Long Trail crossing, Skyline Lodge survives as the lone exception to these protective wilderness rules, the only disturbance to the order of nature in this robust habitat where brilliant clouds and distant peaks reflect between blooming lilies in the ripples of a forest pond.

Skyline Lodge, in the heart of the Bread Loaf Wilderness

The moderate walk to Skyline Lodge begins at Steam Mill Clearing, a well-marked trailhead off Forest Road 59 (FR 59) complete with a campsite, ample parking, and a lookout for wildlife viewing. Striding directly into the shade of the damp New England woods, the Skylight Pond Trail begins a 2.3-mile trek by hopping a brook and ambling another 0.25 mile before crossing a larger stream. Rolling east to begin its 1500-foot ascent of the Green Mountain ridge, the unadorned path soon advances to a signpost and map at the entrance to the Bread Loaf Wilderness. Pitch and elevation steadily mount as the trail wiggles up the slope. Trees take on a tousled look on the breezy upper reaches, but only in the last 0.25 mile do evergreens control the scene as the path zigzags past granite ledges to a 10-yard spur with Champlain Valley views. Always user-friendly, the Skylight Pond Trail avoids the heights of surrounding summits, ending instead at a Long Trail junction in the clearing of a shallow col between Battell and Bread Loaf peaks.

Visitors to Skyline Lodge have no need to lug their overnight gear on ridgeline explorations. Continue straight through the Long Trail clearing and descend the eastern slope. A short spur ends at a classic cabin above an alpine lake with White Mountain sunrise views. One or two paths depart the lodge for openings on the shore, but bushwhacking around this intimate pond is very much discouraged. Leave it to the birds with bustling nests and the moose that guide their young through hidden bogs and private shallows edged by fragrant spruce. Besides, hikers have enough to do. Drop your pack, fill a bottle at a nearby potable spring, and prepare yourself for unfettered hiking on a carefree mountain climb.

Back at the Long Trail junction, hikers have a choice of Green Mountain peaks, with time to climb one or both. For an easy effort, follow the

Long Trail south as it bounces 200 yards uphill to the top of Battell Mountain. Veer west on a 50-yard side path through a crowd of evergreens and tumble down slope to an exposed perch on a rocky outcrop knoll. Don't get too enthralled with the glorious panorama of Lake Champlain, Bread Loaf Mountain, and the Adirondacks of New York. Steep drops and precarious boulders demand close attention as you scramble onto a crag to improve your view in the final jagged yards.

A more elaborate quest awaits hikers on the Long Trail north. Dipping up and down through a series of wetlands on a ridge that links mountain peaks, the white-blazed path quickly arrives at the steepest test of the day, clambering 0.2 mile up the

Climbing Battell Mountain on the Long Trail south

shoulder of Bread Loaf Mountain, highest point in the Bread Loaf Wilderness at 3835 feet. Still cloaked with conifers, the long top of this flat summit extends 0.7 mile through moose bog, sorrel, and fern as an easy walk rambles to a well-signed hairpin turn at the end of your Long Trail hike. Leave the trail at the apex of the curve, keep walking straight ahead, and follow an unmarked path that weaves 0.1 mile between trees to another scenic opening on a second boulder ledge. Noticeably higher than Battell's perch, the vista from the Bread Loaf outlook still captures the sweeping grandeur of the Adirondacks and Champlain Valley. But the scope of the panorama expands to include ski slopes that pop into view and a phalanx of peaks that range north and south from the core of the Green Mountain chain.

Bread Loaf Mountain lends its name to a nearby campus of Middlebury College and a well-known writer's conference. Academics, literary folk, or any average naturalist with a slight poetic bent should know that the drive to the Skyline trailhead enters the realm of Robert Frost. After hiking back to your car, search out the cabin where this pride of New England worked for 23 years, and look for the special interpretive trail where his poems are placed in earthy context just a mile west of the Bread Loaf campus on Highway 125.

The practical guide

Access: Vermont Highway 125 runs east-west between US Highway 7 in Middlebury and Vermont Highway 100 in Hancock. From Highway 125 turn north on Forest Road 59 just 0.3 mile west of the center of the Bread Loaf Campus of Middlebury College, or three miles east of the village of Ripton. The well-marked forest road skirts the edge of the Bread Loaf campus. Follow FR 59 3.6 miles to the Skylight Pond Trail and parking at Steam Mill Clearing.

Accommodations and reservations: First come, first served, but there's usually room for just one more. Bring sleeping bag, foam pad, cook stove, and food. Water and pit toilet are in the area; tent platforms are also nearby for classic backpacking treks. During summer and fall, a caretaker may be on duty to collect a fee for overnight use of the lodge. At this writing, the fee is just $4 for overnight.

Maps: USGS Bread Loaf and Lincoln quads

For further information: Green Mountain National Forest, Middlebury Ranger District, Route 7, RR 4, Box 1260, Middlebury, VT 05753, Tel. (802) 388-4362; Green Mountain Club, Route 100, RR 1, Box 650, Waterbury Center, VT 05677, Tel. (802) 244-7037.

30. SKYLINE LODGE

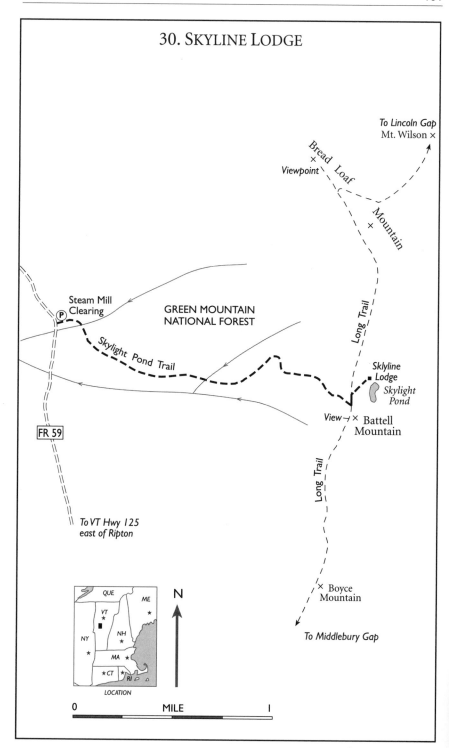

To Lincoln Gap
Mt. Wilson ×

Bread Loaf

Viewpoint ×

Mountain ×

Long Trail

Steam Mill
Clearing
P

GREEN MOUNTAIN
NATIONAL FOREST

Skylight Pond Trail

Sklyline
■ Lodge
Skylight
Pond

View ⌐ × Battell
Mountain

FR 59

Long Trail

To VT Hwy 125
east of Ripton

× Boyce
Mountain

To Middlebury Gap

QUE
ME
VT ★
NY ★
NH ★
MA ★
★ CT ★
RI

LOCATION

N

0   MILE   1

Index

Abol Beach 43
Acadia Hotel 22
Acadia National Park 18, 20–22
A Century Past B & B 76, 79
Action Airlines 122
Adams, Mount 81–83, 92, 94
Alexandria 69
Allagash Lake 24–28
Allagash Mountain 26
Allagash Wilderness Waterway 24, 25, 28, 34
Alpine Trail 132, 133
AMC High Cabin 72
Androscoggin River 107–09
Appalachia trailhead 82, 95
Appalachian Mountain Club 50, 54, 57, 69, 81, 92, 95, 115
Appalachian Trail 7, 40–42, 53–55, 87, 92, 115
Applecheek Farm 144
Arlington 124, 125, 127, 128
Arlington Inn 126, 128
Asticou Inn 22
Atlantic Flyway 5, 118
Atlantic Ocean 20, 36, 59, 117, 120

Bailey Island 52
Baker Island 18
Balmy Days III 47
Bamforth Ridge Trail 133
Bangor 21
Bar Harbor 18, 19, 21, 22
Bar Harbor Hotel-Bluenose Inn 22
Bar Harbor Inn 22
Barr Hill 146
Bascom Lodge 53, 54, 56, 57
Bass Harbor 22
Bass Harbor Head Light 18, 20
Bath 44, 49, 52
Battell Mountain 157–59
Battenkill Inn 126, 128
Battenkill River 124–27
Baxter, Percival 40
Baxter State Park 40–43
Bay State Cruise Company 63
Beal Island 50
Bedell Bridge 76, 77

Belvidere 141, 143, 144
Benedict Bridge 127
Berkshire 150
Berkshire mountains 65
Berlin 103, 105, 107, 109
Bethel Point 51, 52
Bethel Point B&B 51, 52
Big Hen Island 51
Big Hosmer Pond 146
Big Niagara Falls 42
Birch Meadow campsite 78
Bishopsgate Inn 16
black bear 4
Black Falls Brook 151
black flies 5
Black Lantern Inn 150, 152
Black River 146
Black Rock Point 119
Blackhead cliff 45
Blackhead Trail 45
Blackwoods Campground 19, 21, 22
Block Island 117–21
Block Island Airlines 122
Block Island Chamber of Commerce 122
Block Island National Wildlife Refuge 118, 120
Block Island Sound 117, 120
Bloodroot Gap 137
Bloodroot Mountain 137
Blue Dory B & B 122
Blueberry Hill Inn 138, 139
Bond, Mount 89
Bondcliff mountain 89
Bondcliff Trail 88, 89
Bonds, the 86, 87
Boothbay Harbor 47
Boston Island 50
Bradford 77, 79
Brandon 136, 138
Brandon Gap 135, 136, 139
Brassknocker B&B 146, 148
Bread Loaf Mountain 157–59
Bread Loaf Wilderness 157–59
Bristol 69, 73
Brunswick 49, 52
Burnthead 46
Busby Trail 67

Cadillac Mountain 18–20, 22
Calkinstown Road 9

Camel's Hump 130–33
Camel's Hump State Park 130
Cape Air 63
Cape Cod 59, 61, 62
Cape Cod Bay 59, 61
Cape Cod Canal 62
Cape Cod Chamber of Commerce 63
Cape Cod National Seashore 59, 63
Card Cove 51
Cardigan, Mount 69–72
Cardigan Lodge 69–73
Cardigan Reservation 69, 73
Cardigan State Park 69, 73
Carleton Bridge 52
Carmel, Mount 136
Caspian Lake 146, 147
Catamount Trail 135–38, 145, 146
Catamount Trail Association 135, 139, 148
Catamount Trail Guidebook 135
Cathedral Forest Trail 72
Caucomgomoc Checkpoint 27
Caucomgomoc Lake 28, 32, 34
Caucomgomoc Stream 32, 33
Chamberlain Lake 24
Champlain, Samuel de 18
Chapman Pond 15
Charlemont 65, 68
Chatham 59
Chester/Hadlyme ferry 14–16
Chesuncook Lake 30–32
Chesuncook Lake House 30, 32, 33
Chesuncook Village 30–32
Chittenden 139
Chittenden Reservoir 135, 136
Churchill House Inn 138, 139
Cilley's Cave 70
Circular Trail 55
Civilian Conservation Corps 53
Clark Mountain 66
Clark Trail 71, 72
Clay Brook 78
Clay Head Nature Trail 120

Clay Head Swamp 120
Cliff Trail 46
Cobble Mountain 8
Cobscook Bay 36, 37
Cobscook Bay State Park 36–39
Cold Hollow Llamas 142–44
Cold Hollow Mountains 141, 142, 149
Cold River 65
Colebrook, NH 103
Connecticut River 13–15, 75
Connecticut River Valley 75, 76, 79
Contoocook Lake 99
Contoocook Marsh Recreation Area 99
Contoocook River 99
Cook's Corner 52
Couching Lion Farm 130
Country Goose B&B 11
Crafstbury B&B on Wylie Hill 146, 148
Craftsbury Common 145, 146, 148
Craftsbury Inn 146, 148
Craftsbury Nordic Ski Center 145–48
Craftsbury Outdoor Center 146–48
Craftsbury Village 145, 146, 148
Crag Camp (Mount Cardigan) 71
Crag Camp (White Mountains) 81–84
Cranberry Isles 21
Crane Mill Road 37
Crawford Notch 86, 112
Crescent Beach 119
Cundy's Harbor 49, 51
Cundy's Point 51
Currier and Ives 97

Daicey Pond 40–43
Danbury 7, 10
Darwin, Charles 117
Dean Trail 130, 131
Debonis Cutback 137
Debsconeag Checkpoint 33
Debsconeag Gate 43
Deep River 13–16
Deep River Navigation Company 16
Deerfield River 65, 67
Deer Hill Falls 55
Deer Run 137
Dennysville 36, 38, 39

Dogfish Head 50
Dorset 125
Doubletop Mountain 42
Duck Pond 147
Durand Ridge 81

East Craftsbury 146
East Harbor Creek 61
Eastman Creek 77
Eastport 36
East Thetford 79
Ebencook Harbor 50
Echo Lake 20
Edmands Col 81–83
1890 Colonial B&B 11
Ellsworth 21
Emerson, Ralph W. 97
Emily Winthrop Miles Wildlife Sanctuary 9
Equinox Hotel 127
Equinox, Mount 127
Errol, NH 107, 109
Ethan Allen, Mount 131
Ethan Pond 88, 115
Ethan Pond Trail 89, 113, 114
Eustasia Island 14

Fairlee 77, 79
Fallsway 93
Fife'N Drum Inn and Restaurant 11
Firescrew Mountain 70, 71
Fitzwilliam 97
Fitzwilliam Inn 98, 101
Five Islands 50
Florida 65, 68
Folsom's Air Service 34
Forestry Trail 130–33
Foster Field 43
Fowler River Road 73
Franconia Notch 86, 112
Franconia Ridge 86
Franklin Pierce College 99
Frenchman Bay 18, 19, 21
Fresh Pond 118–20
Frost, Robert 159
Fuller Bridge 151
Fuller Mountain Road 8
Furnace Brook 137

Galilee 121
Gelston House 16
Georgetown 49, 52
Gero Island 31–33
Giardia lamblia 5
Gibbs House B&B 11
Gillette Castle 14, 16

Golden Road 27, 30, 32–34
Goose Rock Passage 50
Gorham 81, 92, 95, 109
Gorham Lodge 133
Gorham Mountain 21
Goshen Mountain 137
Gothic B & B 122
Grassy Pond Trail 42
Gray Knob 81–84
Gray Knob Trail 82, 83
Great Barrington 10
Great Cliff 136
Great Gulf 83, 94
Great Salt Pond 119, 120
Green Mountains 130
Green Mountain Club 132, 157, 160
Green Mountain Expeditions 144
Green Mountain National Forest 135, 157, 160
Green River 53
Greenville 24, 27
Greenway 118, 120
Grey Havens Inn 50–52
Greylock, Mount 53–56
Griffith's Head 51
Groton, Lake 155
Groton State Forest 154–56
Groveton 105
Gulf of Maine 51
Gull Cove 46
Guyot Mountain 88
Guyot Shelter 86–89

H2Outfitters 51, 52
Hallowell Flowage 38
Hanging Ledges 70
Hanover 79
Hardy Boat 47
Hazens Notch State Park 151
Head of the Meadows Beach 59, 60, 62
Herring Cove Beach 62
Hewitt Brook 137
Hewitt Brook Run 136
Highland Light 59, 61
Highland Lodge 146, 148
Hildene Meadows 125
Hill Farm Inn 126, 128
Hilltop Pond 8
Hitchcock Corners 9
Hitchcock House 47
Hockomock Bay 50
Holbrook House 22
Holt Clark Cut-off Trail 71, 72

Holt Trail 71, 72
Hoosac plateau 67
Hoosac Range 65
Hoosac Tunnel 68
Hoosic River 53
Hopkins Bridge 150
Hopper 54–56
Hopper Trail 54–56
Hotel Manisses 122
Housatonic Meadows State
   Park 10, 11
Housatonic River 7, 10
Housatonic Valley 7
Hull Cove 20, 22
Hunt Trail 42
Hunter Head 19
Hut at Madison Spring 92–
   95
Hut at Zealand Falls 87, 89
   112–15

Inn at Chester 16
Inn At Southwest 22
Inn on Covered Bridge Green
   127, 128
Inn on the Common 146,
   148
Inn on Trout River 144, 149,
   152
International Paper Com-
   pany 103
Interstate Navigation 121
Island Inn 44, 45, 47
Isle au Haut 18
Israel Ridge Trail 83

Jackson Road 9
Jaffrey 97–100
Jaffrey Center 100
Jay Peak 149–51
Jefferson, Mount 81, 83
Jefferson House 144
Jefferson Ravine 83, 94
Jeffersonville, VT 143, 144
Jewett, Savannah 150
Jewett, Sheldon 150
Jigger III 121
Johnson Pond 24
Jordan Pond 20
Jordan Pond House 20

Kancamagus Highway 86,
   87
Katahdin, Mount 30, 32, 40–
   42
Keeler Road 10
Kennebec River 52
Kent 7, 8

Kettle Pond 156
Kiln Brook 137
King Ravine 81, 82
Knibloc Hill 8, 9
Knibloc Hill Road 8
Knife Edge Trail 40
Knubble Bay 50
Kokadjo, Maine 27

Lakes-of-the-Clouds hut 94,
   95
Lake Umbagog National
   Wildlife Refuge 107–10
Lamoille River 142
Lanesborough, MA 56
Laraway Mountain 142, 143
Ledge Falls 43
Ledyard Canoe Club 79
Lend-A-Hand Trail 87
Lilac Inn 136, 137, 139
Lincoln, Robert Todd 125
Lincoln Woods Trail 86
Link 82
Litchfield Hills 7
Little Hosmer Pond 146
Little Niagara Falls 42
llama treking 141
Lobster Cove Road 47
Lobster Lake 30
Log Cabin 82, 84
Long Island Sound 75
Long Mountain 105
Long Point Light 62
Long Pond 146
Long Trail 151, 130–33, 139,
   142, 157–59
Longley Bridge 150
Loon Lodge 24, 25, 27, 28
Lost Horizon Trail 137
Lost Pond 42
Lowe, Charles 81
Lowe's Path 81–84
Lowe's store 84
Lubec 36, 39
Lyme 79
Lyme disease 5

Macedonia Brook 7
Macedonia Brook Road 8
Macedonia Brook State Park
   7, 8, 10, 11
Madison Gulf 94
Madison, Mount 82, 92–95
Madison Spring 81, 83, 94
Magalloway River 107, 108
Magurrewock River 38
Maine Island Trail Associa-
   tion (MITA) 51, 52

Malden Island 50
Manana Island 46
Manchester 124, 125, 127,
   128
Manning Trail 70, 71
Mannsview Inn 144
Mansion Beach 120
Marathon Trail 146
March Cataract 55
March Cataract Trail 55
Massachusetts Department
   of Environmental Manage-
   ment 54
Matagammon Gatehouse 42
Maze 120
McBurnie, Bert and Maggie
   30, 34
Mendon 139
Middlebury College 159, 160
Mill Covered Bridge 142
Millinocket 25, 27, 40, 41,
   43
Missisquoi River 149–51
Mohawk Trail 65, 66, 68
Mohawk Trail State Forest
   65–68
Mohegan Bluffs 120
Mohegan cliffs 121
Monadnock Inn 100, 101
Monadnock, Mount 97, 100,
   101
Monadnock Region 97
Monadnock State Park 100,
   101
Money Brook Falls 55, 56
Money Brook Trail 55, 56
Monhegan Boat Line 47
Monhegan House 44, 47
Monhegan Island 44–47
Monhegan Light 46
Monhegan Village 44
Montclair Glen Lodge 131,
   133
Montgomery 149–51
Montgomery Center 144,
   149, 151
Monticello Lawn 83
Montpelier 130
Montpelier-Wells River Rail-
   road 155
moose 4
Moosehead Lake 30
Moosehorn National Wildlife
   Refuge 36, 37, 39
Morey, Lake 78
Morgan Bridge 142
mosquitoes 5
Mountain Top Inn & Resort

136–38
Mount Desert Island 18–22
Mount Greylock State Reservation 53, 56, 57
Mowglis Trail 71
mud season 4
Muscongus Bay 44

Narragansett 121
Nash Stream State Forest 103
Nature Conservancy 14, 15, 117, 118, 122
Nauset Beach 59
Nesowadnehunk Stream 40, 42, 43
New Boston Trail 137
New England Air Lines 122
New England Cartographics 57
New Harbor 47
Newbury 75, 76, 79
Newport 117
North Adams 53, 56, 65
North East Carry 30, 32
Northeast Harbor 20
Northeast Kingdom 145–47
Northeast Kingdom Llama Expeditions 144
Northern Vermont Llama Co.
North Light 120
North Maine Woods 24, 27
North Pond 68
North Thetford 75, 76, 78, 79
North Trail 37
North Truro 60, 63
Nowell, Dr. William 81
Nowell Ridge 81
Noyes Pond 154, 155
Nutmeg State 7

Ocean Trail 20
Old Harbor 117, 118, 120, 122
Old Harbor Life Saving Museum 61, 62
Old Jaffrey Meeting House 100
Orford 75–79
Orr's Island 52
Orvis 125
Osgood Trail 94
Otter Point 19–22
Overlook Trail 54, 55
Owl's Head 156

Parapet 94

Parapet Trail 94
Paris Base 104–06
Park Loop Road 19, 20, 22
Passamaquoddy Bay 36
Payne Overlook 121
Peacham Bog 156
Pearly Pond 99
Pebble Beach 46
Pemigewasset Wilderness 86 -89, 112
Penobscot River, West Branch 27, 30, 32, 41
Perch 83, 84
Perimeter Road 42, 43
Phillips Brook 105
Phillips Brook Backcountry Recreation Area 103, 104, 106
Phillips Brook Lodge 104, 106
Phillips Pond 104, 106
Phineas Swann B&B 149, 152
Piermont, NH 77, 79
Pilgrim Mounument 61
Pilgrims 62
Pine Stream 30, 33
Pinkham Notch 94, 95
Pinkham Notch Visitor Center 95
Pioneer Valley 66, 67
Plymouth, NH 69
Point Judith, RI 118, 121
Polis, Joe 31
Pool Pond 99
Port Clyde 47
Precipice Trail 20
Presidential Peaks 92, 94
Presidential Range 81
Pretty Marsh 20
Prospect, Mount 55, 56
Province Lands Visitor Center 63
Provincetown 59–63
Provincetown Airport 63
Provincetown Chamber of Commerce 63
Provincetown Harbor 61
Provincetown Inn 62, 63

Quahog Bay 49, 51
Quarry Knob campsite 14
Quay Path 82, 83
Quoddy Head State Park 38, 39

Race Point 59–63
Race Point Beach 60, 62

Rainy Day Books 99
Randolph 81
Randolph Mountain Club 81, 84
Randolph Path 82–84
Raspberry Island 51
Ravine of the Castles 83
Red Mill Fishing Access 127
Reid State Park 51
Resort Air 122
Rhododendron State Park 97, 98, 101
Richford 151
Ridley Cove 51
Rimrock 72
Rindge, NH 99
Ripogenous Dam 31
Roaring Brook 55
Robinhood Cove 50
Rockefeller, John D., Jr. 20
Rockland, Maine 44, 47
Rockwell, Norman 127
Rodman's Hollow 119
Rose Farm Inn 122
Round Pond 25, 27, 28
Roy Swamp Wildlife Management Area 9
Rutland 135, 139

Sachem Pond 118, 120
Salt Meadow Marsh 60
Salt Pond Visitor Center 63
Samal, Bill 141
Samal, Laurie 141, 142
Sand Beach 19, 20, 22
Sandy Point 120
Sargent Mountain 20
Savoy Mountain State Forest 65, 67, 68
Schoodic Point 18, 21
Seal Harbor 20
Seal Ledges 46
Seawall 18, 20
Seawall Campground 21, 22
Selden Creek 13–14
Selden Island 13–16
Selden Neck State Park 13, 14, 16
Sentinel Mountain 42
Settlers Rock 120
Seyon Ranch 154–56
Seyon Recreation Area 154, 156
Sharon 9
Sharon Motor Lodge 9, 11
Sheepscot Bay 49–51
Sheepscot River 50
Sheffield House 122

Shining Sails 47
Shoal Pond 115
Silver Lake 138
Skyland Trail 71
Skylight Pond 157
Skylight Pond Trail 158
Skyline Lodge 157, 158
Slaughter Brook 42
Smith, Ansel 30
Smuggler's Notch 141, 143, 144
Smutty Nose island 46, 47
Snow Island 51
Snyder Brook 93
Somes Sound 18, 20, 22
Somesville 20
Southeast Light 120
South Hollow Vineyard B&B 63
South Peak 72
South Peak, Guyot Mountain 89
South Pond 67, 68
South Trail 37, 39
South Twin Mountain 87
Southwest Harbor 22
Sperry Campground 55
Spring Island 50
Spruce Mountain 154
Spruce Road 67
Squeaker Cove 45
Staples Brook 67
Stark 105
Star Lake 94, 95
Star Lake Trail 94
Steam Mill Clearing 158
Stockbridge 10
Stone House Inn 78, 79
Stony Ledge 55, 56
Stowe 141, 143
Stowe Llama Ranch 144
Stratford House Inn 22
Sunderland 125, 126

Telos Road 33, 34
Thoreau Falls 112, 114
Thoreau, Henry David 30, 31, 59, 61, 97
Tidswell Point 108
Timberland Trails, Inc. 103, 106
Todd Mountain 65–67
Todd's Point 51
Togue Pond Gate 42, 43
Totem Trail 66
Tote Road 43
Trailing Yew 47
Tribler Cottage 47

Trio Ponds 105
Trout Brook 66
Trout River 149, 150
Truro 59
Twin Mountain 84, 86, 89, 112, 115
Twinway Trail 87–89, 113, 114
Tyler Swamp 68

Umbagog, Lake 107–09
Umbagog Lake Campground 108–10
Umbazooksus Stream 31, 33, 34
Underhill campsite 77
Underhill Trail 46
Upper Ammonoosuc River 106
Upper Valley Land Trust 77, 79
U.S. Fish and Wildlife Service 107, 110
U.S. Life Saving Service 62

Valley Way 81, 93–95
Vaughan Meadow 77
Vermont Association of Snow Travelers (VAST) 137–39
Vermont Department of Fish and Wildlife 126, 128
Vermont Department of Forests, Parks and Recreation 154, 156
Vermont, Lake 130, 149
Vermont Valley 125
Viking Lines 121
Vistamont Trail 71

Wagon Wheel fishing access 126
Waits River 77
Walden Pond 65
War Memorial Tower 54
Washington, Mount 92, 94
Waterbury 130
Waterville 143
Weber Road 8, 10
Wellington State Park 70
Wells River, South Branch 154
Welton Falls 70
West Arlington 127
West Bond mountain 89
West Cornwall 7, 10
West Cornwall Road 9
Westerly 121, 122
West Quoddy Head 38

West Woods Road 10
Whalebone Cove 15
Whalebone Creek 15
Whitcomb Mountain 104, 105
White Cross Trail 100
White Dot Trail 100
White Goose Inn 77–79
Whitehead cliffs 46
White Hollow Road 9
White Mountain National Forest 81, 86, 92, 103, 105, 112
White Mountains 81, 86, 92, 103, 112
White River Junction, VT 75
Whitewall Brook 112, 114
Whitewall Mountain 88, 112–14
Whiting 38, 39
Whiting Bay 36, 38
Whitman Island 51
Wilder 75
Wilder Dam 76, 79
Wilderness Trail 86
Willey Range 88
Willey's Store 147
Williams, Mount 56
Williamstown 53
Wind Gap 131, 132
Wiscasset 47
Woodbound Inn 99, 101
Wood End Light 62, 63
Woodsville, NH 75, 79

Yarmouth Island 51

Zeacliff Junction 88
Zeacliff Pond 88
Zealand Campground 115
Zealand Falls 87, 112–14
Zealand Mountain 88
Zealand Notch 87, 88, 112–14
Zealand Pond 89, 113, 114
Zealand Ridge 87, 88, 114
Zealand River 112, 113
Zealand Road 112, 115
Zealand Trail 112, 113